DAVID THORNE
I'LL GO HOME THEN; IT'S WARM AND HAS CHAIRS
THE UNPUBLISHED EMAILS

ISBN 978-0-615-61595-0
Title I'll Go Home Then; It's Warm and Has Chairs.
The Unpublished Emails.
Contact david@27bslash6.com

Second Edition | published Dec 2012

Also available - The Internet Is A Playground
The Internet is a Playground is the first New York Times best selling book by David
Thorne. It includes the complete collection of articles from 27bslash6 plus over 160
pages of new material. It makes a nice present, protects against tigers, and can be
read while hiding in small places.

For Seb, Holly, Further and Laika

Free Bookmark
Simply fold along dotted line to bookmark this page.

Contents

The title of the book again for some reason 1
Some text and a free bookmark 2
Contents page 3
Contents continued because I ran out of room on this page 4
Foreword 5
Halogen Lamp 10
Arguments 16
Dear Customer 26
Ten reasons I probably shouldn't be alive #1 35
The Battle of Hastings 1066
Our People 40
Ten formal complaints 41
Seventeen reasons not to ask the Internet for advice 63
Bill tries to buy cheese part 1 70
Simon's credit card number 5424 1811 8236 0120
Opinions 71
Bill tries to buy cheese part 2 86
Ten reasons I probably shouldn't be alive #2 87
Two fat ladies 88
The Fibonacci Sequence 1, 1, 2, 3, 5, 8, 13, 21, 34, 55, 89
Penguin appreciates your cooperation 91
Ten reasons I probably shouldn't be alive #3 105
Sexy centrefold 108
David and his best friends go for a drive 110
Timesheets 111
Don't shoot yourself accidently in the head moron 121
Ten reasons I probably shouldn't be alive #4 127
Bill tries to buy cheese part 3 132
Lunch Order Form 133
Kevin's Party 140
Ten reasons I probably shouldn't be alive #5 141
Space 1999 and other Christmas Classics 142
Employee Self Evaluation Form 145
More statements my offspring has made 149
Canada Goose 150
Watch 151
David and his best friends go camping 156

A bit of an emergency 158

Bob's Artwork 159

Ten reasons I probably shouldn't be alive #6 165

The annoying horn thing in the grill procedure 169

Kotex 173

Aliens and Dogs 183

Ten reasons I probably shouldn't be alive #7 187

The Walking Dead 188

Staff weekend 191

David and his best friends go shopping 196

Brochure redesign 198

Chris 206

Moon buggies 209

Ten reasons I probably shouldn't be alive #8 217

Formal Notice 219

Comcast 220

Bill tries to buy cheese part 4 226

Absolute zero .... -273

Literary agents 227

Sodium Chloride 300mg

About the Author 236

Emergency 911

David and his best friends at the end of the book 241

Foreword

Hello. Thank you for buying this book. I apologise for the fact that it isn't as thick as the first one. I probably should have made the type larger or written more, but you know how it is. With round the clock episodes of Property Virgins on HGTV and sleeping to do, there never seems enough hours in the day. Rather than go to any real effort, I thought it would be easier to simply collect all the material I have written that didn't make it into the first book, either due to timing, space, legal issues, or not being very good, and put them in this one.

Hosting fees are expensive. As public interest in what I write has a limited shelflife and it is only a matter of time before people rediscover fun family activities like slip'n'slide and Jenga, I figured I should probably make as much cash as possible while I can. I assumed when Penguin picked up the first book, I would shortly be spending my days shopping for Range Rovers or relaxing on solid gold deckchairs by my swimming pool but this was not the case. There is less money in writing than there is working in the design industry and I am not clever enough to come up with a way of making money with less effort.

I saw a movie once called Lock, Stock and Two Smoking Barrels in which one of the guys had an idea to make money by placing an ad in specialist magazines for a super orgasm inducing vibrator for thirty dollars - cheques made payable to TSF Ltd. After the money is collected, a reply is sent saying there has been a problem with deliveries and they receive a refund cheque from another company called Butt Tickler Dildos Ltd or something. Less than half the people will hand that cheque into their bank to be cashed.

I was watching the movie with my friend Mark and he said, "I would put the cheque in the bank" so I asked, "Does that mean you would buy a super orgasm inducing vibrator from a magazine?" and he replied, "No, I would just drive to a shop and buy one. Or buy an electric toothbrush from the supermarket and take the bristle bit off and put a carrot on it instead." Which is kind of weird and shows he had thought about this previously. I stopped hanging around Mark a few years later when he went on a health kick, gave up drugs, and, after discovering yoga, felt it was important to discuss yoga at every opportunity. It didn't matter what the conversation was about, yoga was the answer. I once asked him his opinion regarding a Pantone colour swatch and although the answer wasn't yoga, I could tell he was thinking about yoga at the time.

A lot has happened since the last book was published, I have changed jobs, moved countries, and married.

I do not have the best track record in regards to previous relationships and despite readily admitting to exceeding others tolerances, up until recently my choices could be construed as anything but wise. My last girlfriend turned out to be a bar fighter, the one before that tried to shoot me with a scuba gun and the one prior to that joined an amateur acting group and made attend her opening of The Importance of Being Earnest. As I felt it was appropriately important to be earnest, when she asked me what I thought of the performance I told her the truth and had to make the fifteen kilometre journey home on foot.

I met Holly while we were both attending a NASA space camp for adults. Helping her to the infirmary, after dropping an auxiliary detonation pipe on her foot, we struck up a friendship in the waiting room and spent the next few weeks partnered for EVA simulations and multi-axis training.

When I asked Holly to marry me two years later, her first reaction was "Why, because I am the only person who will put up with your bullshit?" but followed this with a yes. We were in the bathroom at the time, as she was blow drying her hair after taking a bath, and I felt it was as good a romantic moment as any. Placing the engagement ring on her finger, her other hand still holding the hair-dryer, I gave her a tight hug - sandwiching the hair-dryer between us.

Unfortunately, as she had been using the hair-dryer only seconds before, the front metal grill was almost red from heat and seared into her stomach, branding it with what looked like a target, just above her navel.

Screaming, Holly leapt backwards, tripped over the toilet behind her, and fell. Attempting to stop her descent, she grabbed the shower curtain. While the curtain fabric and hooks held, the bolts securing the rail to the wall did not and the curtain, rail, several wall tiles, Holly, and the hair-dryer she was still holding, fell into the bath.

Really, it was her fault for not emptying the bath when she got out. I have seen in movies where someone drops a toaster in the bathtub and they are electrocuted but it must be houses that don't have a flip-switch fuse system. The instant the hair-dryer touched the water, the fuses flipped and the bathroom was plunged into darkness. Asking "Are you ok?" was met with a crash as the hair-dryer struck the wall near to where Holly had thought my voice had come from, and the reply, "I fucking hate you."

Margin note:

I used to work with a guy named Lucius who told me that pleasing women is easy. The trick, apparently, is to "treat them badly all the time and then when it is their birthday or something, you don't have to do anything apart from letting up on them a bit. Maybe say their hair looks nice. It saves you having to buy presents and stuff and keeps them keen."

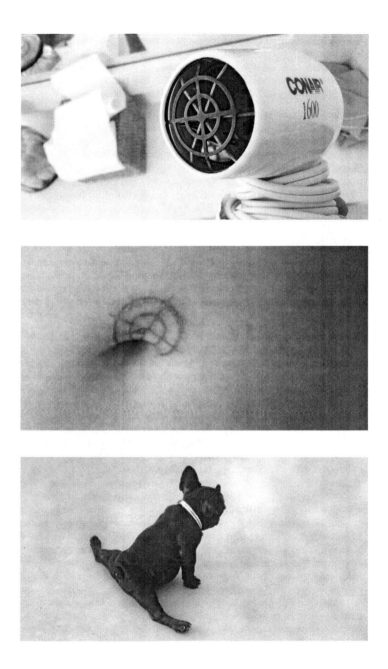

Even a year later, the target shaped scar, which I quite like and view as a permanent reminder of the day she said yes, is constantly used against me. Last week when we were out at dinner with people from her work, I mentioned that she had eaten the last bread roll and she replied "At least I didn't burn and try to electrocute you."

People love watching an argument though so I'm sure everyone had a great time. Once, while I was being interviewed via phone live for some obscure American radio station called NPR, the journalist asked if Holly found me annoying or amusing. Answering that it was the latter, Holly yelled from the living room, clearly audible to the presenter and listeners, "Don't fucking lie." The presenter asked me "Was that Holly?" to which I replied, "No, it was the television" and Holly yelled out again "No it wasn't." Apparently she was cross because I had just ordered an expensive watch for myself from Amazon. It wasn't the fact that I bought the watch, the one I had worn for the last fifteen years was on its last legs, it was the fact that I hadn't ordered her something of equal value. At least that is my analysis. She said it was because we were meant to be saving for a house but I have found since that if I say "I ordered something on Amazon today and ordered something for you too," she doesn't get anywhere near as cross.

Before meeting Holly, I never had a problem with saving as I simply didn't bother with it. I like things. Not lots of things, just certain nice things that I can look at now and then and comment on how nice they are. There wasn't really anything I wanted that required saving for. Living by myself, I only needed a chair so I bought a Herman Miller Eames lounge. The price tag meant I couldn't afford any other furniture, like a bed, but the foot-stool allowed me to use the chair to sleep in and provided a second seat for guests just in case anyone said "I might go and visit David even though he hasn't got any furniture. Or a fridge." When I did buy a fridge, I bought a Smeg because it looked nice but I couldn't afford food after buying a Smeg so I left it unplugged and used it to stack books in. Now that I am married, and have things like bar stools, milk and a dog, priorities have changed and saving for a house has taken precedence. It doesn't have to be an expensive house, just something 'open concept' with a large living area that opens out onto a deck that overlooks woods and perhaps a pond or river with ducks. With steps going down to a pool. And a tennis court. And a dirt-bike track. Design-wise, something like Frank Lloyd Wright's Fallingwater but with less mould. I'm estimating our monthly repayments will be more than I make in a year so I have been looking for a second job for Holly. If you are hiring, send me an email. She complains less than 20% of any given hour, can lift medium sized objects, and can follow a simple set of instructions unless they are for assembly of Ikea products.

Speaking of houses, Ikea products, and New York Times bestselling books, did I mention that the first book made the New York Times Bestseller list? Many lulz were had. It was as much a shock to my publisher as it was to me and a source of crossface for those featured in the book; I received letters from three separate lawyers and a letter from Simon Edhouse pretending to be a lawyer. Around the same time, a relative named Christopher developed an obsessive hatred towards me. As his online crusade to bring me down consisted mainly of changing my Wikipedia page to say "David is gay" he was given the same amount of attention as the lawyers and ignored completely.

I have been accused of pointless irresponsibility when publishing content, in particular the emails, but I have never claimed either responsibility or pointyness. Providing content that encourages argument, discussion and factions structured around humour, rather than simply offending, has always been my goal. While it may appear that the majority of emails I receive are negative, the "I am offended" emails are usually in regards to my "disgraceful and cruel attitude towards cats" and cat owners are insane so I ignore them. I also ignore emails sent from New Zealand. The narrow emotional ledge on which New Zealanders squat may have a grand view but nothing good can come from communicating with these people.

Up until recently, the concept that someone might take their anger out on me beyond the virtual world didn't concern me at all. I lived by myself on the eighth floor of a concrete fortress and promises of retaliation were scoffed at. Having moved into a 'normal' house, I have become more wary. After I tried exchanging defective snowboard gloves and was rudely denied, I created a newspaper ad stating that the store was giving away 4,600 snowboard packages. Apparently, they received over 5000 calls that weekend which resulted in the owner turning up at my premises yelling, so I bought a gun. It's a Nerf gun, but if you stick pins into the ends of the foam darts, they can do some serious damage.

I met a guy named Nick recently who showed me his large collection of guns. He also showed me his bunker and food cache "for when society collapses due to a huge solar flare hitting the Earth and knocking out the grid" so having the gun will probably come in quite handy if Nick is right and I need to take his stuff.

Also, just so this foreword has some form of informative point rather than being simply a collection of vaguely connected paragraphs, the title on the cover of this book is from a statement my offspring made while we were at the park playing football after I used the term "Go hard or go home."

Regards, David.

Dear neighbour,

Due to your new terawatt floodlight shining through our bedroom window like a small but intense sun, I have removed the lamp and placed it in your letterbox.

Regards, David.

david@27bslash6.com

a. "dear god, what's happening?...is that a floodlight?

b. our bedroom window.

c. a dog.

road

I can't help it if some of the light goes across the road.

The photo above of my neighbour Justin plugging in his electric leaf-blower is the best I could get without being caught. I had to take the picture using the digital zoom from between venetian blinds so I apologise for the quality. I'm not Annie Leibovitz. I did not get along very well with my neighbours in Australia and seventeen thousand miles away, little has changed. The fat redheaded family to our right have a fat redheaded dog that enjoys standing in our driveway and barking at 2am, the old couple to our left have never been seen unless you count glancing towards their house and seeing their blinds close quickly, and Justin across the road recently installed a spotlight on his front porch facing directly towards our bedroom window. As we are moving in a few weeks to larger premises with less neighbours, the last night we are here I intend to shoot the fat redheaded dog with a paint-ball gun, moon the old couple, and steal everything in Justin's front yard that isn't bolted down because that is pretty much standard operating procedure in Australia.

From: Justin Flecker
Date: Sunday 6 May 2012 6.52pm
To: David Thorne
Subject: Lamp

I received your note but you cant go onto other peoples property and take things, that's trespassing. Massanutten is a wooded area and I installed that light for security. It's a safety issue. I can't help it if some of the light goes across the road, close your curtains if it bothers you.

....

From: David Thorne
Date: Sunday 6 May 2012 7.41pm
To: Justin Flecker
Subject: Re: Lamp

Hello Justin,

Thank you for your email. While I accept that curtains are usually the key to community accord, in this instance they would need to be constructed of eight-inch-thick lead sheeting.

Last night, with my curtains closed and bedside light off, I read a book. Wearing sunglasses. Under a blanket.

Though unconvinced that blinding local fauna is the best solution, I do understand the heightened need for security living in a wooded area such as the gated community of Massanutten demands. Having formerly lived my entire life in Australia, I am unfamiliar with much of the local wildlife but I did see my first raccoon last week. I stepped outside to have a cigarette and the raccoon, sitting less than five feet away beside an up-ended bin eating the remains of a Domino's Artisan Tuscan Salami pizza, hissed at me. Surprised, I threw myself backwards, rolled several times toward the door, and sprang to my feet holding the welcome-mat above my head to appear taller. Sometime during the roll-spring-mat maneuver, probably during the roll part as it was over gravel and I was wearing shorts and a thin t-shirt so I had to take it slow, the raccoon left. Which probably isn't as exciting a story as it should be but this isn't Borneo and I'm not Jack London.

I did see a snake the other day though. I picked up a stick to poke it with which also turned out to be a snake. Jumping back in panic, I threw it away from me, but our dog thought I was playing fetch and I had to run and jump over a creek to get away.

As such, this weekend I intend to set up a canister of poisonous gas in my yard with an industrial fan behind it. I can't help it if some of the gas goes across the road.

Regards, David.

....

From: Justin Flecker
Date: Monday 7 May 2012 2.14pm
To: David Thorne
Subject: Re: Re: Lamp

Is that meant to be a threat? Put something up in your window if you don't like the light, we lived here 5 years before you even moved into the neighborhood and got along perfectly with Ryan who lived at your property before you. We went to his BBQ's and I loaned him our mower. We get along with all our neighbors. I dont know what you people do in your own country but in this country we dont go onto other peoples property and touch their stuff.

From: David Thorne
Date: Monday 7 May 2012 3.37pm
To: Justin Flecker
Subject: Re: Re: Re: Lamp

Dear Justin,

In my country, terawatt globes are reserved for police helicopter chases and warning sailors of hazardous shoals. This is despite the fact that practically every living creature there can kill you in under three minutes. Our primary spoken language is screaming.

I'm not surprised you get along well with all the other neighbours. If you put fifty children with Down's syndrome in a room there is going to be a lot of hugging.

And no, it was not a threat. It was an exaggerated response to an uncompromising stance. I was taught never to make a threat unless you are prepared to carry it out and I am not a fan of carrying anything. Even watching other people carrying things makes me uncomfortable. Mainly because of the possibility they may ask me to help.

I did consider installing a floodlight as bright as yours, but this would require some form of carrying things, electrical wiring knowledge, and access to a power supply capable of producing that amount of wattage. Probably fusion. As I am told off by my partner for wasting money when I leave the light on in the bathroom overnight, I can only speculate to what her reaction would be to an electricity bill eight times our annual income for retaliatory garden lighting. She would probably have to get a third job.

It would be much cheaper to stand in my driveway and throw rocks. I can't help it if some of the rocks go across the road. You should probably put something up in your window.

Regards, David.

....

From: Justin Flecker
Date: Tuesday 8 May 2012 10.01am
To: David Thorne
Subject: Re: Re: Re: Re: Lamp

Did you take our lamp again asshole? What part about not being allowed to go on our property don't you get?

From: David Thorne
Date: Tuesday 8 May 2012 10.32am
To: Justin Flecker
Subject: Re: Re: Re: Re: Re: Lamp

Dear Justin,

No, I did not take the light again. I relocated it again. Its current location may be discovered by deciphering the following set of clues to its whereabouts. Perhaps you could invite your friend Ryan over and treat it as a kind of treasure hunt:

1. It's in the letterbox again.

2. Look in the letterbox.

As I realise this probably won't narrow it down much for you, I will give you a third clue in the form of a riddle:

What burns with the light of a thousand suns and is in the letterbox?

Regards, David.

From: Justin Flecker
Date: Tuesday 8 May 2012 11.15am
To: David Thorne
Subject: Re: Re: Re: Re: Re: Re: Lamp

I put a smaller lamp in so you can shut the fuck up now. Don't email me again and if you ever trespass on our property again I will press charges.

From: David Thorne
Date: Tuesday 8 2012 12.02pm
To: Justin Flecker
Subject: Re: Re: Re: Re: Re: Re: Re: Lamp

Dear Justin,

What if I have a barbecue and need to send you an invitation? Is it ok to email you then?

Regards, David.

From: Justin Flecker
Date: Tuesday 8 May 2012 12.18pm
To: David Thorne
Subject: Re: Re: Re: Re: Re: Re: Re: Re: Lamp

No it's not ok.

....

From: David Thorne
Date: Tuesday 8 May 2012 12.27pm
To: Justin Flecker
Subject: Re: Re: Re: Re: Re: Re: Re: Re: Re: Lamp

Dear Justin,

What if I need to borrow your lawn-mower? I can't invite people over for a barbecue and expect them to stand in long grass. Someone might be bitten by a snake. It's a safety issue.

Regards, David.

....

From: Justin Flecker
Date: Tuesday 8 May 2012 3.26pm
To: David Thorne
Subject: Re: Re: Re: Re: Re: Re: Re: Re: Re: Re: Lamp

Fuck off back to Austria.

Things Holly and I have argued about this week

Last Friday, while Holly and I were having drinks with another couple, Holly stated that she and I never argue. "That's not true," I said, "We argue every day."

"Don't lie," Holly responded, "that's not arguing, that's just you being a dickhead."

As such, I decided to write down every argument that Holly and I have this week to prove, contrary to Holly's statement, I actually show an impressive degree of patience, self restraint and logic when presented with the exact opposite.

Rocks

On Saturday, Holly and I argued about gardening despite neither of us being in our late seventies. Earlier that morning, she had announced that she was going to build a rock garden on the bare patch of lawn in our backyard.

When Holly is bored and has nothing to do, it usually affects me in horrific ways such as being forced to play Trivial Pursuit or taking the dog for a walk so, as I had a lot of work to do that day, I replied "That sounds like a good idea." Within twenty minutes I was consigned to carrying rocks and piling them a few metres from where Holly planned to build her rock garden.

"Wouldn't it make more sense for me to place them where you want in the rock garden?" I asked. "No," Holly replied, "then when someone visits and says, 'I like your rock garden' I wouldn't be able to say I built it myself."

"You're not building it yourself," I countered, "I'm the one digging up rocks and carrying them, you are just pointing at which rocks you want."

"If I had some kind of machine that could lift the rocks for me then I wouldn't need you," she argued, "you're not contributing to the design, you're just a tool. Like a shovel or a wheelbarrow."

Slightly annoyed at this, I left Holly to it. A few hours later, she declared her rock garden complete and that I should come marvel at it and shower her with praise.

In the middle of the lawn stood a small pile of rocks. I saw a documentary once about Vikings and it showed them burying their dead by piling rocks on top of the body. The rock garden looked like a Viking grave for a cat or possibly a small dog.

"Wow," I said and meant it. "So, no ferns then?"

"It doesn't need ferns," Holly replied looking annoyed. "It's a rock garden, not a rock and fern garden."

"I'm no gardening expert," I ventured, "but I'm fairly certain rock gardens are allowed to include plants. Perhaps just one or two to counter the whole 'Viking baby grave' thing..."

"The whole what?" asked Holly. "Don't take this the wrong way" I went on, "It looks great, but don't you think it maybe, just a little bit, looks like a Viking grave?"

"What do Vikings have to do with gardening?" Holly spat. "It's not a fucking boat."

A few days later, Holly's parents visited and as they walked into the backyard, her father asked, "Why is there a pile of rocks on your lawn? Are you going to make a rock garden?" And her mother added, "You should be careful when you move them, snakes like living in places like that."

Nacho Soup

Holly cannot cook. She is capable of the process of cooking, but Holly cannot cook in the same way that an octopus cannot ride a bike; it has enough arms to reach the pedals and handlebars but the result will rarely be a successful journey from A to B.

I once looked over Holly's shoulder to discover her crumbling Alka-Seltzer tablets into a meal she was preparing because "they are salty and we ran out of salt."

Saturday evening, Holly stated that she was making nachos for dinner so I was surprised to be presented with a bowl and spoon an hour later. "What's this? I asked.

"The nachos were a bit runny so I added a few cups of water. It's nacho soup," she replied.

"Is there even such a thing?" I asked. "And what are these bits in it?"

"They're the chips," Holly replied defensively as she sipped a spoon of Nachos and made a long "mmmmmm" noise. "I put it all in the blender so there shouldn't be any big bits."

"I'm ringing for pizza," I said.

"Typical," replied Holly, "you never appreciate anything I do."

"That's not true" I responded, "I appreciate everything you do but if I ordered a hamburger at McDonald's and they handed it to me in a cup with a straw saying 'Sorry, it was a bit runny so we threw it in the blender and added two cups of water, it's Big Mac soup', I would assume the restaurant was entirely staffed through some kind of special needs employment initiative. If they asked me, "Do you want fries with that?" I sure as fuck wouldn't reply, 'Yes, mix them in.'"

"It would probably be quite good," responded Holly, "but you would never know because you are too much of an asshole to taste it. Even if the guy at McDonalds spent an hour in the kitchen making it for you and burnt his thumb on a saucepan."

"Fine," I relented, taking a scoop and raising it to my mouth, "I'll taste it." Sipping at the brown and yellow puree, I felt an intense burning sensation not unlike having a mouth full of red ants. I swallowed with effort as my eyes began to water and said, "It's a bit spicy."

"Yes," said Holly, "We were out of Cumin so I used Curry instead. It's like an Indian version of Nacho soup."

Vanna White

When I wake up before Holly, usually to let the dog out so it doesn't take a dump on the kitchen floor, I make her a coffee and take it to her in bed whispering, "Time to wake up, you have to get ready for work," or "Time to wake up, the dog took a dump on the kitchen floor and it isn't going to clean itself up."

On one occasion, I whispered, "The police are here. If they ask, I was home last night and you don't know anything about Mr O'Brian's cows."

Sunday morning, Holly woke me up by punching me in the neck.

Thinking that someone was attacking me, perhaps a burglar or an evil doll that had come to life, I rolled away from the blow and out of bed yelling, "What? What's happening?" Holly, staring at me from in bed, said, "I had a dream you had sex with Vanna White."

Groggy and still puzzled as to what was happening, I asked, "Who the fuck is Vanna White?"

"She's the lady that turns the letters around on Wheel of Fortune," Holly replied, "I dreamt you were having an affair with her and I came home and she was wearing my clothes."

"What the fuck?" I asked, "She's in her eighties."

"So if it had been someone younger that would be ok would it?" Holly demanded. "No," I replied as I dressed, "but if I am going to get punched in the neck because you have a dream about me having an affair, I would rather it be with someone born after the Civil War."

"Like Kate Beckinsale? You love her don't you," Holly accused. "What?" I responded, "I've never even met her."

"Yes, well," continued Holly, "You've never met Vanna White either and that didn't stop you."

Making my way out of the bedroom as quickly as possible, I walked downstairs to make a much-needed cup of coffee and discovered the dog had taken a dump on the kitchen floor.

Motorbikes

I recently bought a dirt bike. A YZ250F for those interested in such things. To justify buying the motorbike, I told Holly that it was for her. "If you learn to ride," I said, "I will buy a second bigger one for myself and we can go riding together on trails." On Sunday afternoon, we drove to a secluded area in the forest and unloaded the bike.

"What's this button do? asked Holly as she hopped on, "Is that to start it?"

"That's a bolt. You have to kick start it," I replied, showing her how to put it in neutral and start the engine.

"Where's the accelerator?" asked Holly.

"You twist the right-hand grip," I answered, "And it's not called an accelerator on a motorbike, it's called a throttle."

"Well that's just stupid, I'm going to call it an accelerator," responded Holly.

"If you are not going to take this seriously you probably shouldn't..."

"I am taking it seriously," Holly cut in, "You're not the boss of names. Just show me how to make it go. If you can ride a motorbike it can't be rocket science."

"Ok, fine," I said, "Squeeze the clutch and put it in gear. No, you press down for first..."

"So the clutch is called a clutch and the accelerator is called something stupid?" Holly interrupted, "Why didn't they just call the clutch a squeezer?"

"What?" I replied, "It doesn't matter what it's called, you have to squeeze the clutch and release it slowly as you increase the thro... the accelerator. It's exactly the same process as driving a manual car."

"I'm going to call it a squeezer from now on," stated Holly, "So I just twist the whatsit and let go of the squeezer?"

"Well, yes," I answered, "But you have to release the squeezer slowly and twist the accelerator at the same time otherwise the bike will stall. And if you give it too much accelerator and let go of the squeezer too quickly, it will take off and you will probably crash."

"Ok," said Holly as she twisted the throttle to maximum and let go of the clutch to give me a 'thumbs up'.

The bike tore forward and Holly, now horizontal and screaming, travelled about twenty metres with the throttle in a death grip before developing speed wobble and being thrown off. The bike flipped a few times before coming to a halt.

Running towards her, I saw Holly climb unsteadily to her feet, hold out her arms as if doing an impression of a plane caught in turbulence, then fall over again. Kneeling at her side and asking if she was ok, Holly turned to me, focused, and said, "You are a terrible fucking teacher."

Breaking Bad

On occasion, I have to work late due to the time difference between the US and Australia. On Sunday evening, Holly was watching a program called Breaking Bad in bed while I was working in the next room. Not realising I was on the phone with a client, she yelled "We should build a Meth-lab in the garage."

Mammoths

Four years ago, Holly asked me to laminate a news clipping of a cat that had adopted a mouse. Inserting the clipping, which featured a photo of a cat and mouse sleeping in a basket with the caption 'Purrfect Parenting' as Holly watched on excitedly, it came out the other end with a dead fly between the layers. Apparently I had done this on purpose.

On Monday morning I walked into the kitchen to find Holly making toast. I generally feel safe eating toast that Holly has made because it requires minimal ingredients to forget, replace or experiment with, but this toast was a bit thin and soggy.

"It's a bit thin and soggy," I said, "what bread is this?"

"It's the same bread we always have," Holly replied, pointing to the bag.

"I didn't even know we had any brea...oh my god," I exclaimed, "it has a best-before date of January 2009."

"It was in the freezer," Holly said defensively, "The best before date doesn't count if the product is frozen."

"I'm fairly sure there is a limit," I responded holding up a slice of bread consisting almost entirely of permafrost.

"No there isn't," Holly replied, "I saw a show once where scientists found a Mammoth frozen in ice for millions of years. They thawed it out, cooked it and ate it. "

"That didn't happen," I replied, "You told me once that you saw a show about a man who ate his own head and it turned out to be an animated gif. Why would scientists eat a mammoth?"

"Because they are scientists," said Holly, "and they know a lot more about science and how long things can be frozen for and still be eaten than you do. You don't even know how to use a laminating machine."

Staring as Holly raised a thin soggy piece of toast to her mouth and took a bite, she chewed and added thoughtfully, "I like mammoths. I wish we had one. A small one, for the dog to play with."

Underpants

More than three years ago, I wore a pair of Holly's underpants because I had run out of clean pairs of my own. I will admit to wearing them the next day as well because they were all spandexy, but that is twice only once a long time ago.

While having dinner with Holly's parents on Monday night, her mother stated, "I was watching a program about Hitler last night and apparently he liked dressing up in women's clothing."

"Really?" Holly replied, "David likes wearing women's underpants."

The Milk Carton

On Tuesday morning, Holly and I argued about where the milk carton should be kept in the fridge. I often work from home and while I don't need a desk or filing cabinet (as I work from a laptop), I do have one working requirement: Coffee. I drink around twenty cups of coffee per day and I have milk in my coffee.

My valid suggestion that the milk should live in the door, where it is readily accessible to the person who uses it most, was countered by Holly's anarchic opinion that "the milk doesn't have a special milk spot in the fridge. Its special spot is wherever I put it."

The fact that I drink a lot of coffee was also quickly hijacked. As we own a Keurig, which uses little plastic coffee buckets that work out to around a dollar-fifty per coffee, Holly calculated that my daily consumption of twenty cups amounted to forty-five dollars. She then used an actual calculator and admitted it was closer to thirty dollars but that it was still "a ridiculous waste of money."

Ignoring my justification of coffee being a 'tool of my trade', Holly began pounding keys on the calculator and spouting numbers such as "That's two-hundred and ten dollars per week... eight-hundred and forty dollars per month... ten-thousand and eighty dollars per year... We could buy a car with that money."

"Yes, to live in," I responded, "because without coffee I wouldn't get any work done and I wouldn't get paid; we should probably buy a station-wagon or perhaps a camper-van. Even then it might be cramped, what with the dog and..."

"I work as well," Holly interrupted, "It would only be you living in the car, the dog would stay here with me. You can take the Keurig."

"Fine," I replied, "I will live in a car by myself and within a day you will call and say, '''Im bored and want to play Trivial Pursuit. I was going to watch television but the garage door keeps opening when I try to change channels. Come home.' and I will reply, 'No, sorry, I like living in the Waffle House carpark.'"

"That won't happen," Holly responded, "I will be way too busy putting the milk wherever the fuck I want."

Also, while on the subject of Keurigs, when it is out of water, I take the reservoir out, fill it, and replace it. This way there is enough water for the next person and several more coffees. On the rare occasion Holly finds the Keurig empty, she fills a cup with water, takes the lid off the Keurig machine, pours the cup in, and makes a single coffee. When I was at school, I was taught that 'good manners are contagious' but this is clearly bullshit.

Liam Neeson

I arrived home Tuesday afternoon to discover a framed photo of our dog on our living room wall. I like our dog but when I am home, so is the dog. I don't need to see photos of it. Especially if the photo shows the dog siting on the couch that is immediately below the framed photo and the dog is actually sitting on that couch at the time.

Sitting down next to the dog, I grabbed a magazine from the coffee table and flicked through until I came to an interview with actor Liam Neeson. The facing page featured a photo of Mr Neeson in a suit, sitting on a chair with one leg crossed over the other, holding a glass of red wine. Ripping out the page, I replaced the photo of the dog in the frame with it.

Arriving home a short time later, it took Holly less than fifteen seconds to storm into the kitchen brandishing the frame and demanding, "What the fuck is this?"

"It's Golden Globe award winning actor Liam Neeson," I replied.

"Yes, I know who Liam Neeson is," Holly responded, "Where's the dog?"

"It's sitting on the couch," I replied, "It's always sitting on the couch. And having a photo above the couch of it doing so is weird. We may as well put a photo on the wall of all three of us sitting on the couch and then sit on the couch and look at it. Or put up a mirror."

As she stormed back out in search of the missing photo, Holly said over her shoulder, "It's not as weird as having a photo of Liam Neeson on the wall."

"I like Liam Neeson," I replied.

"Well I like the fucking dog," Holly yelled back, "If you love Liam Neeson so much why don't you marry him instead. Then you can put up hundreds of photos of him."

Which is a ridiculous statement because if I was married to Liam Neeson and saw him everyday, I obviously wouldn't need photos of him on the wall to look at. Also, if I was married to Liam Neeson and we had a bare wall, we could probably afford a professional interior designer who knew what they were doing.

House Hunters

On Tuesday night, Holly and I watched a program on American television called House Hunters in which couples look at three houses and then buy one. You are probably thinking, "that sounds pretty entertaining," but you are wrong and much better off watching How It's Made or Storage Wars. Even American Pickers is a better show, you just have to keep your finger primed on the remote to change channels in case their bush-pig female assistant makes an appearance.

"Can we watch How It's Made or Storage Wars instead?" I asked.

"No," Holly replied, "You will like this one, it's the International version and the couple are buying a house in Australia."

"I've been there," I replied, "I've never been to a storage auction."

"Well I've never been to a factory that makes springs," Holly declared, "but that doesn't mean I want to watch a fucking show about it."

Shaving Cream

Our shower cubicle contains around three hundred items. Two of these items, a can of shaving cream and a razor, are mine. The other items are bottles and tubes of various shape, colour and size containing moisturisers, gels, scrubs, masks, body wash, face wash, and things with mysterious names such as Pro-X. Even though the shower cubicle is fairly large, there is actually only about one square foot of space in which to stand and spin.

While I was shaving in the shower Wednesday morning, Holly walked into the bathroom and stared at me with a shocked look on her face. "What?" I asked.

"Just how much shaving cream do you use?" She demanded, "I could hear the 'pshhhhhhhhhh' noise going on for about ten seconds. Even people with normal sized heads don't use that much."

Pumpkins

Halloween is not celebrated In Australia. While dressing up is common, it has nothing to do with pumpkins and often involves changing quickly in panic as your partner pulls up unexpectedly in the driveway. Decorating your front yard is another thing that isn't done in Australia for reasons I have already mentioned. Once, while living in Adelaide, I woke up to find someone had taken my lawn.

For my first Halloween party in America last year, I went to some lengths to make what I thought was a reasonable Ron Burgundy outfit but was asked several times, "Are you meant to be Borat?" This year I will probably just wear a hat or something.

Left it too late to construct a costume for that upcoming Halloween party? Simply photocopy the image (enlarging 1200%), cut around the lines indicated, and attach a piece of string.

Free Oprah Winfrey Halloween Mask

On Wednesday afternoon, Holly reminded me that Halloween is only a week away and that we still hadn't decorated. It was quickly decided that my suggestion of "sticking the plastic skeleton we bought last year on the porch again" was a "piss poor" one and that I should drive to the supermarket and buy three pumpkins instead.

Returning and carrying the pumpkins inside, Holly stared at them in horror and asked "Is this a joke?"

"What's wrong with them?" I asked.

"Look at them," declared Holly, throwing out her hands towards the pumpkins like an angry Price is Right model, "That one is all bendy, that one is a squash, and that one looks like a bird has been pecking at it. What am I supposed to do with them? We can't put them out the front of our house, people will drive past and say, 'they obviously don't give a fuck.'"

"You could make soup out of them," I suggested.

A few hours later, I stepped outside to have a cigarette and discovered the plastic skeleton sitting in a chair on our front lawn. It was wearing my only suit, had one leg crossed over the other, and was holding a glass of red wine.

Plastic Skeletons

This morning, Holly woke me up yelling that someone had stolen our plastic skeleton. There was no coffee or whispering involved.

"We should call the police," Holly declared.

"Yes, probably," I replied climbing out of bed, "I've no doubt they have a special task force dedicated to tracking down missing Halloween decorations. Make sure you give them a detailed description and tell them you want the front lawn dusted for fingerprints."

"We could drive around and look for it," suggested Holly.

"Ok," I agreed, "I'll check the bus station while you post missing plastic skeleton posters on poles."

"Did you know that whenever you say something sarcastic, you do this little thing with your mouth as if you are repeating what you said silently?" asked Holly, "It's as if you think what you said was so fucking hilarious, you want to run through it again."

"It's in the fucking shed." I replied.

events is necessary, argues

26

Dear customer,
I hope you fall and break
your neck.

As an Australian currently living in the United States, I have been lucky enough to experience many things previously unavailable to me. Although I still flick the switches the wrong way, think the electrical outlets look upset and cringe whenever the word aluminium is pronounced, I have fallen in love with many of the things I assume most Americans take for granted - like snow and having four actual seasons.

The four seasons in Australia consist of "fuck it's hot," "Can you believe how fucking hot it is?", "I won't be in today because it is too fucking hot" and "Yes, the dinner plate size spiders come inside to escape from the heat. That is a fucking whopper though."

I hate spiders. If I am reincarnated as a spider, I will bite myself and not seek medical assistance. Once, while I was at work, a spider ran up my arm. I threw myself backwards onto the floor and rolled around while thrashing and undressing to make sure the spider was not in my hair or clothes. Unfortunately I was in a client meeting at the time with a company that sells cleaning products.

If the meeting had gone better I probably could have got a good price on a Dyson. I have actually only seen one spider in the entire time I have been in the US and it was the size of a well sucked on m&m. I flicked it into the sink. In Australia, the presence of a spider involves combat gear and improvised weapons.

I do miss aspects of Australia though. Not many but aspects nonetheless. I would kill for a packet of Arnott's Pizza shapes and I saw an episode of Oprah recently where she flew the entire audience to Australia to listen to Russell Crowe sing which brought a tear to my eye. It was that bad.

My favourite aspect of the United States is the snow. While those around me complain of sliding off the road and having to shovel paths, I quietly hope ten thousand inches are dumped overnight forcing everyone to dig tunnels to Waffle House and snowboard to Wal-Mart.

From: anton@function4sports.com
Date: Thursday 20 January 2011 11.14am
To: David Thorne
Subject: Advertisement

I received a snowboard advertisement from a friend who follows you on twitter or something. If this was some kind of joke I fail to see the humour. We had over 5000 calls asking for free snowboards and I know you are responsible.

From: David Thorne
Date: Thursday 20 January 2011 12.26pm
To: anton@function4sports.com
Subject: Re: Advertisement

Dear Anton,

Thank you for your email. I have been called many things while staying in the US, including 'foggot' and 'youreonthewrongsideoftheroadmoron', but having recently seen my first snowfall and immediately heading out to spend several hundred dollars on snowsurfing equipment, I hardly think the label 'responsible' is justified.

Contrary to popular belief, there is not a lot of snow in Australia and I recently discovered two facts; 1. Snow is cold and; 2. Coming from a climate where the coldest winter demands only complaining slightly less about how hot it is, I am ill-equipped for fact 1.

Unfortunately, these discoveries were made half way up a ski-lift while dressed in jeans, a long sleeved t-shirt and soaking wet rental boots in minus twelve degree weather. Reaching the summit and finding myself unable to feel my extremities or bend back into a standing position, I rolled off the lift chair and slid down the embankment on my side before coming to a stop helped by a small group of children.

After assuring the parents that kids get nose bleeds all the time and it was probably more to do with the altitude than my left elbow, I decided to forego that morning's activities, walk down the hill, and sit in my vehicle with the heater on while researching local snow-apparel shops on my iPhone.

Arriving at your store a short time later, I explained to a salesperson that I required warm clothing and "a pair of waterproof gloves for use in the snow." Based on his brand recommendation and assurance that they would perform in the manner required, I purchased a pair of 180s snow gloves, along with several other items of snow related clothing, and ventured back to the slopes. Assuming the gloves would be waterproof for use in the snow (possibly due to being told "these are waterproof gloves for use in the snow") I was surprised to find they became soaked within seconds and bled black ink down my sleeves and all over the front of my jacket.

Returning to the store immediately, brandishing both the result and receipt, I politely stated that I was not seeking compensation for the ruined jacket, just simply wished to exchange the gloves for a pair not designed to destroy everything they come into contact with.

I was told, "Fuck off. You've worn them."

Being that customer service is arguably a company's most valuable asset, I assumed you would appreciate all the free marketing and promotional help you could get.

Regards, David.

From: anton@function4sports.com
Date: Thursday 20 January 2011 4.18pm
To: David Thorne
Subject: Re: Re: Advertisement

You bought gloves and ruined them and then you want to exchange them for a different pair? No store does that. You cant return something already worn. You have no idea about running a business. If I was working that day I would have told you to fuck off too. Dont be surprised if you get a call from the police. Are you going to pay for the extra staff I had to put on to take all the phone calls?

From: David Thorne
Date: Thursday 20 January 2011 5.06pm
To: anton@function4sports.com
Subject: Re: Re: Re: Advertisement

Dear Anton,

I would actually be more surprised if the local constabulary hasn't got me on speed dial by now. And, going by the adage 'You get what you pay for' in regards to the level of expertise and customer service skills your staff display, I doubt the wages for 'extra staff you had to put on' would exceed the $44 I paid for the pair of destructogloves.

The three staff members working the day I purchased the gloves, who I will refer to as Fatty, Tatooey and Fuzzy for identification purposes, seemed rather annoyed by my interruption of their 'sitting in a chair looking cool' time. Fuzzy seemed the most inconvenienced but that is understandable what with having to deal with inappropriate questions such as, "Do you sell waterproof gloves for use in the snow?" in a snow-sports shop.

Although intending to also purchase board, bindings and boots that day in order to avoid dealing with rental-shop queues that make the Perestroika bread lines look like a couple of friends standing around having a chat, I did not wish to infringe any further on Fuzzy's prime duties of growing an awesome beard and showing a rash to Fatty and Tatooey. Although Tattooey provided him with a diagnosis of "dude, don't pick it, let it scab" that could only have stemmed from several years in medical school, Fatty was less than impressed and only gave it a mild glance and noncommittal grunt before going back to playing Angry Birds. I should probably be thankful that your staff were too occupied with having their earlobes stretched by Tonka-truck tyres and wearing pants around their knees to sell me a snowsurfingboard made of sugar or goggles made of bees.

While I may not have your experience running a business, I am pretty sure that if I owned a shop that sold chairs and you entered and said to me, "Hello shopkeeper, I am looking for something to sit on" and I replied "Sure, this one should suit your needs perfectly, it is made for sitting on" and you purchased the chair, took it home, sat on it, and it exploded, taking out previously purchased furniture with it, you would probably drive back to my shop and say, "Excuse me, I bought this chair an hour ago, used it in the manner you recommended, and it exploded - I am not asking for compensation for my other furniture but would like to exchange it for a non-exploding chair that performs in the manner originally described." Responding with anything other than "I do apologise, here's a replacement" would certainly come as a surprise to you and I doubt "Fuck off, you sat in it" would mean I'd see you, Fatty, Tattoey and Fuzzy at my premises the following week shopping for cushions.

Also, quick question: Having seen the publicity photo of you with your staff, I realise you probably use a child's board but what length would you recommend for a normal sized human? What would be ideal is a really wide snowsurfingboard with handles that I can lay down on. Or one with a seat and steering wheel. Perhaps with some kind of caterpillar tread based wheel system and a motor so that you can ride it up the hill instead of having to take the ski-lift.

Regards, David.

From: anton@function4sports.com
Date: Friday 21 January 2011 11.04am
To: David Thorne
Subject: Re: Re: Re: Re: Advertisement

Its snowboarding not snowsurfing and 5"8 isn't short dickwad. I doubt my staff acted in that way but if they did then it is probably because we get hundreds of weekend warriors in here during ski season and we like to know if they are serious or just window shopping before we waste hours helping them.

I'm sick of noobs like you who dont know what they want or shit about snowboarding coming in wasting our time. If I refunded money or exchanged gear to every looser who had a problem with their gloves, I'd be broke.

From: David Thorne
Date: Friday 21 January 2011 2.17pm
To: anton@function4sports.com
Subject: Re: Re: Re: Re: Re: Advertisement

Dear Anton,

Yes, I am pretty sure if I ran a snowboardsurfing shop the last thing I would want is people new to the sport mistakenly entering my premises with the intention of exchanging goods for money. What a bunch of 'loosers'. You should probably have that on your front door instead of the welcome sign. Otherwise, people might read the word 'welcome' and mistakenly think they are welcome. Perhaps you could incorporate a sign similar to the 'You must be this tall to ride' kind displayed at carnivals, but amend it to 'You must be this cool to enter' with a big red arrow pointing to photos of Fatty, Tattooey and Fuzzy.

Also, I apologise. While the average male height of 5"9 statistically means anything under is considered short, my question was without diminutive intention. I'm sure there are many advantages to being so small. Target carries an excellent range of boys clothing at competitive prices and a lower centre of gravity should, once helped up onto the ski-lift, allow you to snowboardsurf with greater stability. If I were small, I would buy a cat and ride it.

I do object to the label 'noob' though. Thirty minutes of watching instructional Youtube videos have to count for something. One of them showed a squirrel water-skiing which is pretty much the same thing so how hard can it be? I am at least twice as intelligent as a squirrel and I once covered almost the entire distance of a slip'n'slide in a standing position so the basic skill set is there. I expect to be doing steezy jumps within the first hour and Olivers by lunch.

When I was nine I attempted to jump my new Standish 12 Selectaspeed racing bike across a creek. Building a ramp from timber removed from an adjoining playground fort, I calculated that a speed of 150mph - based on a previous evening's episode of Knight Rider - would see me safely over the fifteen metre gap. Having also seen episodes of Dukes of Hazzard where they jump bridges and the nose of the General Lee crumples a bit, I strategically placed a pile of leaves on the estimated landing point to soften the impact. In front of an expectant crowd consisting of two kids from the playground and a dog, I rode to the top of a hill, donned my father's welding mask and gloves (safety first) and began the descent.

Overcoming momentary speed wobble somewhere around eleventh gear, I believe I would have made it had the dog not run in front of me at the last moment, causing me to veer and miss the ramp by about four metres. Approximately half way over the creek and realising my trajectory was not going to make the distance, I attempted to pull the bike upwards, a midair bunny hop if you will, resulting in the handlebars separating from the frame.

Somehow, while my bike dropped into the creek, my body managed to make it to the far bank and roll several times before coming to a halt. Jumping to my feet and exclaiming "I'm ok" to my horrified audience, one of them pointed and I looked down to discover a rib poking out of my chest as a red stain slowly spread outwards ruining my Return of the Jedi t-shirt. I also discovered that the dog had, minutes before my approach, defecated in my landing spot. Which for some reason seemed more horrifying to me than the protruding rib at the time. Accepting the loss of Chewbacca and two Ewoks but attempting to remove my shirt before the bloodstain reached Luke, it caught hard on the rib and I blacked out from the pain. During the ambulance ride, I regained consciousness long enough to overhear one of the medics state, "Three broken ribs and a left... is that dog shit?"

While I was recovering in hospital, my father took the bike back to the shop it was purchased from, showed the defective handlebar bolt and described the accident - admittedly omitting the parts about the ramp, creek and dog poo. They replaced it with a new bike and threw in a helmet as way of apology. That store is where I bought my offspring's first, second and third bike twenty years later.

Regards, David.

From: anton@function4sports.com
Date: Friday 21 January 2011 3.37pm
To: David Thorne
Subject: Re: Re: Re: Re: Re: Re: Advertisement

Its ollie not oliver. You really dont have a fucking clue do you. You bought gloves without doing your research first and WORE them and fucked them up and then tried to return them even though we have a sign that says returns are at our discretion. Just because you dont get it doesnt make you right.

I intend to call my lawyer about your stupid advertisement. You are banned from my store and I'm blocking your email address. I'm too busy making 40 grand a week from noobs like you to read your bullshit. Enjoy your gloves dickwad.

From : David Thorne
Date: Friday 21 January 2011 3.51pm
To: anton@function4sports.com
Subject: Re: Re: Re: Re: Re: Re: Re: Advertisement

Dear Anton,

I assumed Ollie is short for Oliver just as Anton is short for a normal sized human. While I appreciate your well wishes in regards to the gloves, I have already replaced them with a pair of black North Face 'Montanas' (for approximately half the price I paid for your 'alarmed squid' squishmittens) from another snowsurfing business named Freestyle who were also happy to recommend and fit a selection of boards, bindings and boots.

You should check them out. They have a lot of good stuff there and I can't recommend them enough. Ask for Justin.

Regards, David.

From: anton@function4sports.com
Date: Friday 21 January 2011 4.09pm
To: David Thorne
Subject: Re: Re: Re: Re: Re: Re: Re: Re: Advertisement

I hope you break your fucking neck in a fall noob.

34

Ten reasons I probably shouldn't be alive:
The rowboat

I watched a show on television recently called *I Shouldn't Be Alive* in which they feature people who, due to things that happened to them, apparently shouldn't be alive. In the episode I watched, some guy was walking along a creek bed and a big rock fell on his leg, trapping him with one foot sticking out. A huge crayfish that lived in the creek crawled out towards him and the guy didn't have a stick or anything in reach to shoo it off with so he had to watch it eat his foot. I would rather the rock had fallen on my head. While I have never had a crayfish eat my foot, I have been on fire, stabbed, lost, almost drowned, crushed and trapped, so here are my own ten reasons why I probably shouldn't be alive.

This article was originally quite long and I thought people might email me saying "tl;dnr" so I broke it up into separate segments and moved them randomly around the book. This was quite annoying as I was pretty much over it by then and it messed with the formatting of other articles so I hope you appreciate the effort and refrain from emailing me asking, "Why didn't you just put all ten reasons you probably shouldn't be alive in one article?"

So, I quite like boats. Many years ago I wanted to buy and live on a boat but after discovering that the only kind of vessel I could afford on my budget was a second-hand rowboat, I gave up on the dream of boat ownership and bought a book about boats instead.

A couple of years before he stabbed me in the stomach, my relative Christopher bought a large, old, wooden rowboat with proceeds raised from a homemade charity collection tin and a week of knocking on neighbour's doors. I still don't understand how he got away with it for so long as both the apostrophe and letter *S* were missing from the words Children's Cancer, but his plan to "do up the rowboat and sell it for heaps" was nothing short of entrepreneurial genius. If Donald Trump ever hears about it he will probably say, "Everyone's fucking fired, I want the rowboat guy."

Paying three hundred dollars for the rowboat, patching the holes with Plaster of Paris, and painting the whole thing white with house paint, the boat was placed in the middle of his front yard with a sign reading "4 SAIL. $1000" . When I mentioned that the word sale was spelled incorrectly, I was told that it was a clever play on words and that is why I didn't get it.

A short time later, Christopher was arrested, on charges I won't go into but involved the attempted sale of a large amount of copper wire to one business and the disappearance of a large amount of copper wire from another, and was sentenced to nine months in Adelaide's Yatala prison. It was about his eighteenth offence. As Christopher rented the property he was living in and couldn't pay the rent while incarcerated, his lease was forfeited and he was given two weeks to remove his possessions.

Being the only relative that owned a trailer, I was somehow delegated the task of removing and storing the rowboat in my shed. Arriving early Saturday morning in order to get the task out of the way and leave the rest of my weekend free, I quickly realised that due to the weight of the boat, I should have brought someone to help me.

I was able to wobble it from side to side on its hull but unable to lift it at all. Positioning the trailer in the driveway parallel to the boat, I came up with the ingenious plan of rocking the boat from side to side until it flipped over onto the trailer, figuring I could get someone to help me drag it off once I was home.

As I began to rock the boat back and forth (A) with increasing momentum, it appeared my plan was working quite well and I managed to get it practically vertical (B) up on its side when I slipped on the grass (C) and fell. Realising the boat was about to roll back on me, I tucked my arms to my sides and rolled away from it as quickly as possible (D), almost making it to safety, but the boat returned to its original position and, carried by it's own momentum (E), continued its arc and flipped over onto me (F).

Pinned face down on the grass by the two planks of wood which made up the seats inside of the boat, one across my back and the other across my legs, I was unable move. I read somewhere once about a lady who managed to lift a tree off her baby or something due to finding untapped strength under stress, or perhaps it was the power of love or something like that. She must have been fairly fit or it must have been a little tree because regardless of how stressed I was feeling about being trapped under a boat, the boat wouldn't budge. It probably only works if there is a baby involved or at least a much loved family pet.

After what seemed like an hour of yelling, "Help, I'm under a boat" proved futile, it dawned on me that the absolute darkness meant the boat's weight had created a fairly solid seal rendering it sound proof. Wiggling my arms, I was able to reach into my pants pockets in search of something useful but the only items I found were my cigarettes and lighter. By twisting my arm into positions it had never been before, probably due to untapped dexterity under stress or the power of love

Margin note:

If I owned a boat (a decent one), I would probably, at least once, re-enact the scene from Titanic where the fat girl stands on the bow with that little guy with the massive head that drowns about seventeen hours into the movie.

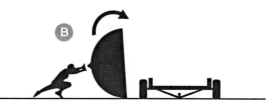

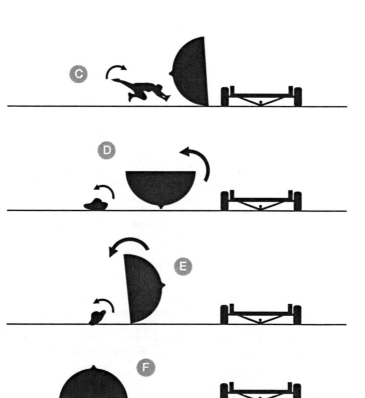

of nicotine, I was able to edge my left hand up to my face and have a cigarette while I pondered my situation.

I actually considered using the lighter to set alight the boat, with the hope that a neighbour might see the smoke and investigate, but the thought of news reports detailing my death by burning to death under Christopher's stupid boat caused logic to kick in. Instead, I banged the lighter against the side of the boat in three bang sequences on the off chance that someone walking past might know morse code and either rush to my rescue or call the authorities.

As I was banging, I struck a section that Christopher had plugged with plaster of paris and a hole the size of a ten cent piece appeared as a section of the makeshift repair popped out the other side of the boat. Elated by Christopher's half-arsed approach to boat repair, I bashed excitedly at the hole and was able to increase its size to double. Manoeuvring my head towards the hole, I looked through and saw the family next door reverse their car down the driveway, with kids in the back, and drive off down the street.

Deciding to wait patiently for their return, at which time I planned to yell through the hole and be rescued, I relaxed and had another cigarette.

Several cigarettes later, and with the sun setting, the neighbours had still not returned and I was becoming quite cross at them. Who goes out for this long? Surely it was past their kids' dinner time and this was irresponsible parenting. Around midnight, I accepted the fact that the neighbours had gone away on a weekend trip.

An hour or so later, I stopped crying and decided that if I was going to escape, it would have to be without aid. As all attempts to lift the boat upwards had failed, my only recourse was to attempt to move the boat horizontally. Digging my fingers and the toes of my shoes into the grass, I strained forwards until my head was hard against the wood at the bow of the boat. Repeating this procedure, while also arching my back against the wooden seats, I felt the boat move forward an inch. Encouraged, I again pushed forward with all my strength and the boat again moved another inch.

Estimating the edge of the lawn to be eight feet from the sidewalk and the sidewalk approximately four feet wide, I calculated that I would have to push the boat another one hundred and forty four times to reach the edge of the curb. At which point I would be able to edge the boat lip over the edge of the curb's drop-off and crawl out.

On push ninety six, I hit the letterbox and had to back up a few inches to go around it but eventually reached the sidewalk and found the boat moved much easier over concrete.

Margin note:

While Holly was reading this page, she asked me "did this really happen or are you just carrying on?" Sadly, there is not only no exaggeration, but I purposely left out details such as having to urinate after about the fifth hour, screaming when I felt a spider web in the dark, and striking deals with god despite being a card-carrying atheist.

The only other time I have been trapped is when my cousin Daryl rolled me up in a rug, wedged me between the wall and a wardrobe, and went home. Four hours later my sister discovered me and poured water down the top of the rug. When my parents returned home a few hours after that, I was smacked for fucking around with the rug and getting it wet.

As the lip of the boat reached the curb, I almost cried with relief as hours had passed and my fingers were numb and bleeding from the process. Gripping the curb's edge, I pulled with all the energy I had left and the boat teetered, then slid, taking me with it, all the way onto the road.

I was now under a boat on the side of the road. Angry and frustrated, I banged against the hull with the palms of my hands and screamed "get off of me, get off of me" until my outburst was suddenly interrupted by the sound of car tyres screeching and a loud thud against the side of the boat; sending it sliding several feet.

Dazed by the knock and grazed by being dragged several feet along asphalt beneath a boat, I heard the sound of a car door closing and a man's voice state, "There's a fucking boat on the road."

After an exchange that included "what the fuck are you doing under a boat" and "there's no way I am going to be able to lift this son of a bitch," the man, who turned out to be a milkman named Tom on his predawn local milk delivery run, managed to raise an edge of the boat by using a tyre iron as leverage and I rolled finally to freedom.

After explaining what happened, thanking him for rescuing me and attempting to hug him (denied due to the copious amounts of blood on my arms and face from sliding several feet underneath a boat along asphalt), Tom said to me, "You know, that's actually a really nice boat."

Several months later, when Christopher asked where his boat was, I told him I had given it to a milkman.

Wyndham&Miller™

Our People / Simon Dempsey

Simon has worked for W&M since 2008 as a potted plant. Popular with the ladies, Simon enjoys knitting leg-warmers for his cats and performing dance extravaganzas for his mother. He is the founding and sole member of *The Dempsey Dance Academy* and meets once a week to discuss late membership fees. His best friend is a dead bee he found on his windowsill in 2004 which he named Simon.

Simon can speak fluent Simonese, a language he developed using only vowels. He is adept at sewing and owns a Singer Stylist 7258. By using a magnifying glass, Simon has created over three-hundred costumes for his bee ranging from jogging outfits to red carpet attire.

Simon's key specialty at W&M is wearing shirts the same color as the walls. He is also an expert at sitting very still. Before joining W&M, Simon held a variety of positions including stretched out, standing on tippy-toes with his hands on his hips, and crouched. Once, when Simon was young, he saw a horse. Simon has a tattoo on his lower back of musician Kenny Rogers riding a bear and has an extensive working knowledge of the latest technologies including metric and Jenga. His favorite music is his own which he creates on his RCA cassette recorder by humming and clapping. Each Friday night, for the last four years, he has invited his neighbors over to listen. Attendance has been disappointing despite the offer of free cabbage.

Simon is currently single but one day hopes to marry his mother because of her "good child-bearing hips." In the meantime, Simon is active on several dating sites under the username *Mr Bobbity*. His last online girlfriend, who he dated off and on for three years, turned out to be an auto-responder.

On weekends, Simon enjoys thermostat regulation, scratching, making lists of things that are blue, and collecting felt. An active member of the community, Simon can often be seen by his neighbors jumping on a trampoline in his back yard. He hopes to one day be a professional trampoliner and has perfected jumping with his arms held at his side, jumping with his arms outstretched, and jumping freestyle.

Simon's career goals are to multiply 1089 x 9 to get 9801 and to establish a floating city in the Pacific Ocean where he will be king and everyone will have to do what he says.

Ten F26-A
formal complaint notices
in six months

Apparently after receiving three complaints, you are meant to have some kind of formal meeting between the parties involved but this never happened. According to the rules, if there are five complaints, an external mediator has to be bought in. This didn't happen either and I was quite disappointed.

I don't really have anything against Simon apart from the fact that he likes the band Nickelback and I have no idea what his problem with me is, as I'm pretty sure I am an absolute pleasure to work with. I brought in donuts once, which is pretty nice. I found them in a bin and left them near Simon's desk. When he asked, "Who brought these donuts in?" I replied, "The girl from the shop across the road brought them in because they have too many" and watched him eat four, complaining between mouthfuls that they weren't very fresh. He would have eaten them all but stopped after finding a dead cricket in the box.

My very first run in with Simon was when he blamed me for stealing pens from his desk, which I vehemently denied. He then proceeded to point out the tiny engraved words 'Simon's Pen' he had done on all eight of the pens currently on my desk.

It was so small he had to point them out to me with the aid of a loupe. Each two-millimetre high letter was meticulous. When I asked how he had managed to get the letters so perfect, he told me that he had a headset at home with a light and magnifying glass on it. When I asked why he had a headset with light and magnifying glass on it he replied, "For painting collector figurines."

There have actually been twelve formal complaints by Simon against me but two of those were complaining that nothing had been done about the previous formal complaints so I didn't bother scanning those in.

F26-A

Date JUN 13 /2011	Date of offense JUNE 13 2011
Name of person filing F26-A SIMON DEMPSEY	
Name/s of person/s involved DAVID THORNE	
Complaint type ☑ Internal ☐ External ☐ Other:	

Description	Ref: ☑ Formal ☐ Med ☐ Class 1 ☐ Class 2

WHILE I WAS AT LUNCH A PACKAGE CAME FOR ME BECAUSE
I ORDERED A T SHIRT ONLINE LAST WEEK. IT WAS ON MY
DESK AND WHEN I OPENED IT THERE WAS A PAIR OF SOCKS IN IT
AND I COULD TELL THE PACKAGE HAD BEEN OPENED AND
TAPED BACK UP. WHEN I WENT INTO DAVID THORNES OFFICE
HE WAS WEARING THE T SHIRT. HE DID NOT HAVE MY PERMI-
SSION TO OPEN THE PACKAGE OR TOUCH MY PERSONAL PROPERTY

Action Requested ☑ Disciplinary ☐ Mediation ☐ Other:

Signature	JUN 13 /2011

Office Use Only	RECEIVED
Ref ☒ F26-A ☐ F26-B Lodged: ☒ Y ☐ N	
F26-B Attached ☐ Y ☒ N Date JUN 13 2011 /2011	

42

F26-A

Date Jul/12/2011	**Date of offense** July 7 2011

Name of person filing F26-A   SIMON DEMPSEY

Name/s of person/s involved   DAVID THORNE

Complaint type [✓] Internal   [ ] External   [ ] Other:

Description   Ref: [✓] Formal   [ ] Med   [ ] Class 1   [ ] Class 2

DAVID THORNE KEEPS ANSWERING THE PHONE BY SAYING HELLO THIS
IS SIMON DEMPSEY. I HAVE ASKED HIM TO STOP BUT HE IS STILL
DOING IT. SCOTT FROM APB RANG AND ASKED FOR A PDF AND
DAVID SAID HE COULDNT DO IT RIGHT AWAY BECAUSE IT IS
TIME FOR HIS NAP. THIS IS UNPROFFESIONAL AND MAKES
ME LOOK BAD TO THE CLIENT. HE ALSO KEEPS SENDING ME
VIDEOS USING PHOTOBOOTH TO MAKE IT LOOK LIKE HE IS ON A
ROLLER COASTER. THIS IS WASTING COMPANY TIME AND INTERNET.

Action Requested [✓] Disciplinary   [ ] Mediation   [ ] Other:

Signature   Jul/12 /2011

Office Use Only

Ref [X] F26-A   [ ] F26-B   **Lodged:** [X] Y [ ] N   RECEIVED

F26-B Attached [ ] Y [X] N   **Date** JUL 12 2011

43

F26-A

Date JULY 15 /2011	Date of offense JULY 15 2011
Name of person filing F26-A SIMON DEMPSEY	
Name/s of person/s involved DAVID THORNE	
Complaint type [✓] Internal [ ] External [ ] Other:	

Description   Ref: [✓] Formal [ ] Med [ ] Class 1 [ ] Class 2

I PUT A TUPPERWARE CONTAINER IN THE FRIDGE THAT
HAD A SANDWICH AND A KITKAT IN IT AND WHEN I OPENED
IT AT LUNCH TIME THERE WAS A PICKLE IN IT INSTEAD. THIS
IS STEALING. I KNOW IT WAS DAVID THORNE BECAUSE HE SAID
I SHOULD GO TO LUNCH EARLY BECAUSE I DESERVE A BREAK TODAY
WHICH IS WHAT THEY SAY IN THE KITKAT ADVERT.
HE DID NOT HAVE PERMISSION TO TAKE MY PROPERTY.

Action Requested [✓] Disciplinary [ ] Mediation [ ] Other:

Signature	JUL / 15 /2011

Office Use Only

RECEIVED

Ref [X] F26-A [ ] F26-B	Lodged: [ ] Y [X] N
F26-B Attached [ ] Y [X] N	Date JUL 15 2011

F26-A

Date AUG 11 / 2011	Date of offense AUG 11 2011

Name of person filing F26-A   SIMON DEMPSEY
Name/s of person/s involved   DAVID THORNE

Complaint type [✓] Internal [ ] External [ ] Other:

Description   Ref: [✓] Formal [ ] Med [ ] Class 1 [ ] Class 2

I HAD 2 BOXES OF BUSINESS CARDS IN MY DESK
DRAWER AND SOMETIME IN THE LAST MONTH DAVID THORNE
REPLACED THEM WITH CARDS THAT HAVE MY TITLE
CHANGED FROM GRAPHIC DESIGNER TO HORSE WHISPERER.
I DONT KNOW WHEN HE CHANGED THEM SO I DONT KNOW
HOW MANY I HAVE GIVEN OUT TO PEOPLE. THIS IS
A WASTE OF COMPANY MONEY AND UMPROFESSIONAL.

Action Requested [✓] Disciplinary [ ] Mediation [ ] Other:

Signature *[signature]*   AUG / 11 / 2011

Office Use Only

| Ref [X] F26-A [ ] F26-B | Lodged: [x] Y [ ] N | RECEIVED |
| F26-B Attached [ ] Y [X] N | Date AUG 11, 2011 / 2011 | |

45

From: Simon Dempsey
Date: Thursday 31 March 2011 12.37pm
To: David Thorne
Subject: No Subject

Did you draw Justin Biebers face on all the images in my stock images folder and save them over my files?

....

From: David Thorne
Date: Thursday 31 March 2011 12.44pm
To: Simon Dempsey
Subject: Re: No Subject

Yes.

....

From: Simon Dempsey
Date: Thursday 31 March 2011 12.49pm
To: David Thorne
Subject: Re: Re: No Subject

What the fuck for? What are you even doing in my files?

....

From: David Thorne
Date: Thursday 31 March 2011 12.56pm
To: Simon Dempsey
Subject: Re: Re: Re: No Subject

I didn't think you would notice. I am meant to be laying out a business card for a client so was looking for a distraction and realised I can open and save files from your computer over the network.

....

From: Simon Dempsey
Date: Thursday 31 March 2011 1.05pm
To: David Thorne
Subject: Re: Re: Re: Re: No Subject

But what did you put Justin Biebers face on them for dickwad? I was going to use them for something.

From: David Thorne
Date: Thursday 31 March 2011 1.12pm
To: Simon Dempsey
Subject: Re: Re: Re: Re: Re: No Subject

You can still use them. Justin Bieber is very popular.

....

From: Simon Dempsey
Date: Thursday 31 March 2011 1.27pm
To: David Thorne
Subject: Re: Re: Re: Re: Re: Re: No Subject

Stay off my computer and you better have a backup of the original images. Do you have a backup?

....

From: David Thorne
Date: Thursday 31 March 2011 1.31pm
To: Simon Dempsey
Subject: Re: Re: Re: Re: Re: Re: Re: No Subject

No.

....

From: Simon Dempsey
Date: Thursday 31 March 2011 1.43pm
To: David Thorne
Subject: Re: Re: Re: Re: Re: Re: Re: No Subject

Right dickhead. I'm making a formal complaint.

F26-A

Date APR 4 / 2011	Date of offense APRIL 4 . 2011

Name of person filing F26-A	SIMON DEMPSEY

Name/s of person/s involved	DAVID THORNE

Complaint type ☑ Internal ☐ External ☐ Other:

Description   Ref: ☑ Formal ☐ Med ☐ Class 1 ☐ Class 2

WHILE I WAS AT LUNCH DAVID THORNE WENT ON MY
COMPUTER OR WENT ON IT OVER THE NETWORK WITHOUT

MY PERMISSION AND HE PHOTOSHOPPED JUSTIN BIEBERS

FACE ONTO ALL THE PHOTOS IN MY PERSONAL STOCK

IMAGES FOLDER . HE DID NOT HAVE MY PERMISSION AND

HE ADMITTED TO DOING IT . THIS IS A WASTE OF COMPANY

TIME AND DAMAGE TO MY PERSONAL PROPERTY .

Action Requested ☑ Disciplinary ☐ Mediation ☐ Other:

Signature	APRI 4 / 2011

Office Use Only

RECEIVED

Ref ☒ F26-A ☐ F26-B	Lodged: ☒ Y ☐ N
F26-B Attached ☐ Y ☒ N	Date / APR 04 2011

F26-A

Date MAY/ 11 /2011	Date of offense MAY /1 2011

Name of person filing F26-A SIMON DEMPSEY

Name/s of person/s involved DAVID THORNE

Complaint type [✓] Internal [ ] External [ ] Other:

Description Ref: [✓] Formal [ ] Med [ ] Class 1 [ ] Class 2

WHILE I WAS DOWNSTAIRS IN THE WIP MEETING DAVID

THORNE PAINTED MY IPHONE WHITE WITH LIQUID PAPER.

THIS IS DAMAGING MY PERSONAL PROPERTY. IT IS THE

3RD TIME HE HAS DAMAGED MY PROPERTY ON PURPOSE.

I KNOW IT WAS HIM BECAUSE BEFORE I WENT INTO THE MEETING

I SAID I WANTED THE NEW WHITE IPHONE. THERE IS LIQUID

PAPER IN THE PLUG THAT THE HEAD PHONES GO INTO.

Action Requested [✓] Disciplinary [ ] Mediation [✓] Other: REPLACE IT

Signature MAY /11 /2011

Office Use Only

RECEIVED

Ref [X] F26-A [ ] F26-B	Lodged: [X] Y [ ] N
F26-B Attached [ ] Y [X] N	Date MAY 12 2011

F26-A

Date MAR 9 / 2011	Date of offense MARCH 9 2011

Name of person filing F26-A	SIMON DEMPSEY

Name/s of person/s involved	DAVID THORNE

Complaint type [✓] Internal [ ] External [ ] Other:

Description   Ref: [✓] Formal [ ] Med [ ] Class 1 [ ] Class 2

WHILE I WAS AWAY YESTERDAY DAVID THORNE MOVED MY

DESK INTO THE KITCHEN AND MOVED THE WATER COOLER AND

BOOKSHELF AND THE BIG PLANT TO WHERE MY DESK WAS AND HE

CHANGED THE PHOTO OF KAREN I HAD IN THE FRAME TO A PHOTO OF

THE FRIDGE. THIS IS TAKING PERSONAL PROPERTY AND WASTING

COMPANY TIME BECAUSE IT TOOK ME 2 HOURS TO MOVE IT ALL

BACK BY MYSELF BECAUSE HE SAID HE WAS TOO BUSY RESEARCHING

WASPS TO HELP.

Action Requested [✓] Disciplinary [ ] Mediation [ ] Other:

Signature   MARCH 9 / 2011

Office Use Only

Ref [X] F26-A [ ] F26-B	Lodged: [X] Y [ ] N	RECEIVED
F26-B Attached [ ] Y [X] N	Date MAR 09 2011	

52

F26-A

Date Feb / 17 / 2011	Date of offense FEB 17 2011

Name of person filing F26-A	SIMON DEMPSEY

Name/s of person/s involved	DAVID THORNE

Complaint type [✓] Internal [ ] External [ ] Other: _____

Description   Ref: [✓] Formal [ ] Med [ ] Class 1 [ ] Class 2

DAVID THORNE CHANGED MY HOME PAGE SO INSTEAD OF GOOGLE

IT GOES TO A MAN SINGING. I DID NOT GIVE HIM PERMISSION

TO GO ON MY COMPUTER. I HAVE CHANGED IT BACK BUT IT KEEPS

HAPPENING. HE ALSO CHANGED THE P AND W KEYS AROUND ON MY

KEYBOARD SO IT OPENS THE PRINT BOX INSTEAD OF CLOSING THE

WINDOW AND THE PLASTIC BIT BROKE OFF WHEN I TRIED TO

CHANGE THEM BACK. THIS IS DAMAGING COMPANY PROPERTY.

Action Requested [✓] Disciplinary [ ] Mediation [ ] Other: _____

Signature _(signature)_   Feb / 17 / 2011

Office Use Only

Ref [✗] F26-A [ ] F26-B   Lodged: [✗] Y [ ] N   RECEIVED

F26-B Attached [ ] Y [✗] N   Date FEB 17 2011

53

F26-A

Date APR 6 / 2011	Date of offense APRIL 6 2011

Name of person filing F26-A SIMON DEMPSEY

Name/s of person/s involved DAVID THORNE

Complaint type ☑ Internal ☐ External ☐ Other:

Description	Ref: ☑ Formal ☐ Med ☐ Class 1 ☐ Class 2

I GOT AN EMAIL FROM LOUISE SAYING THAT I HAD TO PAY
$75 FOR SWIMMING LESSONS BECAUSE IT IS COMPANY SAFETY
REGULATION. WHEN I GAVE HER THE MONEY SHE DIDNT KNOW
ANYTHING ABOUT IT. I KNOW IT WAS DAVID THORNE BECAUSE WHEN
I ASKED HIM IF HE HAD TO DO THE LESSONS AS WELL HE SAID NO
BECAUSE HE SHOWED LOUISE A COPY OF HIS HIGH SCHOOL SWIMMING
CERTIFICATE. BUT THERE ARE NO LESSONS. YOU CANT SEND
EMAILS FROM OTHER PEOPLE. THIS IS FRAUD AND A WASTE OF
COMPANY TIME.

Action Requested ☑ Disciplinary ☐ Mediation ☐ Other:

Signature	APR 6 / 2011

Office Use Only	
Ref ☒ F26-A ☐ F26-B Lodged: ☒ Y ☐ N	RECEIVED
F26-B Attached ☐ Y ☒ N Date APR 06 2011	

F26-A

Date MAR/ 25 / 2011	**Date of offense** MARCH 25 2011

Name of person filing F26-A   SIMON DEMPSEY

Name/s of person/s involved   DAVID THORNE

Complaint type [✓] Internal [✓] External [ ] Other:

Description   Ref: [✓] Formal [ ] Med [ ] Class 1 [ ] Class 2

SOMETIME EITHER THIS MORNING OR LAST NIGHT DAVID THORNE

GLUED PICTURES OF HIS FACE ONTO THE NICKELBACK POSTER ABOVE

MY DESK. HE USED SPRAY ADHESIVE AND WHEN I TRIED TO PEEL THEM

OFF IT RIPPED THE PAPER. THIS IS DAMAGING MY PERSONAL PROPERTY.

HE MUST HAVE SPRAYED ON MY DESK BECAUSE THERE IS A FILM OF

ADHESIVE ALL OVER MY DESK AND MY ARMS STICK TO IT WHEN

I AM USING MY COMPUTER.

Action Requested [✓] Disciplinary [ ] Mediation [ ] Other:

Signature   MAR/ 25 / 2011

Office Use Only

RECEIVED

Ref [✗] F26-A [ ] F26-B   Lodged: [✗] Y [ ] N

F26-B Attached [ ] Y [✗] N   Date MAR 2/5 201 1/2011

55

From: Jennifer Haines
Date: Monday 21 November 2011 9.26am
To: David Thorne
Subject: Meeting this afternoon.

Good morning David,

I hope you had a good weekend. I'm not sure how many client meetings you have today but can we find time this afternoon to have a chat? Simon has filed another formal complaint against you which makes a total of 14 this year. I thought it might be a good idea if all three of us sat down to have an open discussion and try to work towards a resolution.

Jennifer

From: David Thorne
Date: Monday 21 November 2011 9.34am
To: Jennifer Haines
Subject: Re: Meeting this afternoon.

Good morning Jen,

The last time I checked, there were only twelve complaints and two of those were complaining that nothing had been done about the other ten. What are the thirteenth and fourteenth regarding?

Regards, David.

From: Jennifer Haines
Date: Monday 21 November 2011 9.51am
To: David Thorne
Subject: Re: Re: Meeting this afternoon.

Simon filed a F26-A on the 9th of this month stating you had changed his server login ID to Mr Bobbity Head and another on Friday claiming you hacked into his personal Amazon account and ordered a book about boats. He printed screen shots and supplied these with the F26-A. Under section 5, paragraph 2 of the Employee Workplace Agreement which we all signed, I am meant to provide support through discussion of the issue with both parties. Would 2.45 today be ok with you?

Jennifer

From: David Thorne
Date: Monday 21 November 2011 10.14am
To: Jennifer Haines
Subject: Re: Re: Re: Meeting this afternoon.

Dear Jen,

If Simon really took offence to the title Mr Bobbity Head, he would put some effort into stopping it thrashing about as if he is asleep on a roller-coaster. I passed him in the corridor this morning and had to perform a tuck and roll. Providing support through discussion would seem to me less effective than some kind of medical neck brace. Although I received no request from Simon to change his login name, which would possibly have been more appropriate than a formal complaint, to appease his denial of truth, I have amended it to Mr Non-Bobbity Head.

In regards to Simon's Amazon account, my 'hacking' knowledge consists entirely of having seen the movie Sneakers eighteen years ago. Renting an apartment across the street with an unobstructed view of Simon's keyboard through a telescope would require far greater organisational skills than I believe I have ever exhibited while working here. I have three months of unfinished work on my desk and spent last week playing Words with Friends on my phone. As such, it is more likely he simply ordered the book about boats himself and then forgot doing so.

I saw a movie once where Goldie Hawn bumped her head on a boat and got amnesia. Snake Plissken made her look after his kids. It's entirely plausible that, after ordering the book about boats, Simon struck his head during one of his bobbity jaunts down the corridor.

Alternatively, he may have repressed the memory. I have read that repressed memories may sometimes be recovered years or decades after the event, triggered by a particular smell, taste, or suggestion through hypnotism. I am happy to attempt to hypnotise Simon if you think this may help. I will email him now and schedule a time.

Regards, David.

Things Simon has said that annoy me #2

"I just went to make a coffee and there are no k-cups left for the Keurig. We had a box of 50 and I counted the used ones in the bin and there is 16 missing. David has a Keurig at home so I think we should be allowed to check his bag each day before he leaves."

From: David Thorne
Date: Monday 21 November 2011 10.18am
To: Simon Dempsey
Subject: pressed memories.

Dear Simon,

Jen and I have been discussing the possibility that you may have Repressed Memory Syndrome and feel it might be helpful to hypnotise you. Would 2.45 today be ok?

Regards, David.

....

From: Simon Dempsey
Date: Monday 21 November 2011 10.26am
To: David Thorne
Subject: Re: pressed memories.

Fuck off dickhead.

....

From: David Thorne
Date: Monday 21 November 2011 11.22am
To: Jennifer Haines
Subject: Simon's repressed memories

Dear Jen,

Simon seems reluctant to participate. This can often be the case when dealing with motivated forgetting in which a subject blocks out painful or traumatic experiences in his or her life. I wish I had the ability to block out certain memories of my own. I have attempted to put a recent event behind me for the sake of the company but Simon's continued efforts to make himself out to be a victim have left me with no other recourse than to file a formal complaint myself.

On Tuesday evening, the 15th of November, I stayed late to start a project the client was expecting to see the next day. I had been given the project a fortnight prior but this was around the same time I downloaded Words with Friends. Simon was the only other person left in the office.

Perhaps I should have recognised the signs earlier - comments such as "Those pants are nice," and "What kind of conditioner do you use? Your hair smells like coconut & orchid" - but, having grown up on a small farm, I guess I was simply naive to the ways of city folk.

"That thing about only being able to fold a piece of paper eight times is rubbish. Give me a piece of paper the size of a bed sheet and an industrial metal press, and I could easily double that."

Things Simon has said that annoy me #3

I was in the middle of writing copy concerning the lifestyle merits of choosing galvanised roofing materials when the lights dimmed and I heard Justin Timberlake's SexyBack coming from Simon's work area. I looked up to discover Simon dancing slowly in the doorway. I asked what he was doing but he stepped towards me, placed a finger to my lips, and stated, "Simon says shhh little one. This is not the time for words." I attempted to explain that it was and the client was expecting four pages of them by the next day but he wouldn't listen and straddled my chair.

Confused and alarmed, I attempted to push him off but, despite what you would assume from a complete absence of any muscle tone, he was stronger than me and pinned my arms firmly against the armrests, kissed my neck, and whispered, "I can be gentle, or very very rough. The choice is yours."

Not being overly happy with either option, I pushed hard against the desk with my legs, sending the chair rolling across the room before careening into several stacked boxes of Reflex copier paper, toppling the chair and sending us sprawling. Realising this may be my only chance of escape, I tucked my arms to my sides and rolled, like a child on a steep grassy knoll, and leapt to my feet. Bolting out the door and into the dark and stormy night, I heard him crying, "I'm sorry. Come back." But I didn't.

While I accept Simon may be sorry for what he has done, in the interests of protecting fellow co-workers and being compliant with section 5, paragraph 9 of the Employee Workplace Agreement, please find attached a copy of the report.

I request a full investigation into this incident and expect Simon to undertake the sexual harassment course as outlined in Section 3, paragraph 2, of the Employee Workplace Agreement which we all signed. Failing this, a F26-B will be filed with head office as per Section 3, paragraph 8.

Regards, David.

Simon giving oral sex to a whale.

F26-A

Date *Nov / 21 / 2011*	Date of offense *Tue November 15*

Name of person filing F26-A	*David Thorne*
Name/s of person/s involved	*Simon Dempsey*
Complaint type ☐ Internal ☐ External ☒ Other: *Sexual*	

Description	Ref: ☒ Formal ☐ Med ☐ Class 1 ☒ Class 2

It was a dark and stormy night. Justin Timberlake bought sexy back. Simon Dempsey moved to the beat and into my office, silencing first my protests with a finger, then my struggles with a straddle. Though the strength of his desire was greater than my objections, my office floor boards provided a smooth surface and means of escape. I rolled and ran. If my office had been carpeted, who knows how it may have turned out.

Action Requested ☒ Disciplinary ☒ Mediation ☒ Other: *Education*

Signature	*Nov / 21 / 2011*

Office Use Only

Ref ☒ F26-A ☐ F26-B	Lodged: ☒ Y ☐ N	**RECEIVED**	
F26-B Attached ☐ Y ☒ N	Date NOV 21 2011		

From: Jennifer Haines
Date: Monday 21 November 2011 1.45pm
To: David Thorne
Subject: Re: Simon's repressed memories

David,

I really don't have time for you 2 today. Your story is completely unbelievable and filing a class 2 complaint means I am required to provide head office with a completed I-95A assessment and recommendation form. Is this really what you want?

I will have Simon do the TWE course if you retract or change your complaint to class 1 so it can be dealt with internally. Do not send a F26-B to head office. I have no idea what is going on between you two but I would appreciate it if you would sort this nonsense out between yourselves in future without creating more paperwork for me.

Jennifer

Things Simon has said that annoy me #4

"I could easily build a robot with artificial intelligence if I wanted to - if you gave me enough money and a year or two. I pick these things up pretty quickly and I have a huge shed."

From: David Thorne
Date: Monday 21 November 2011 2.02pm
To: Jennifer Haines
Subject: Re: Re: Simon's repressed memories

Dear Jen,

Thank you for your understanding. What happened is indeed completely unbelievable but through the support of those around me I hope to make it through this difficult time. I am not a victim; I am a survivor.

As a long time advocate of education over discipline, and accepting partial responsibility for what occurred as I was wearing nice pants that day and had used Herbal Essence's 'Hello Hydration' 2-in-1 Hawaiian coconut & orchid moisturising shampoo and conditioner that morning, I agree to your request and will amend the complaint to class 1 following Simon's completion of the TWE course. I also accept your position on wasting company resources through misuse of the F26-A form for matters that would be better dealt with through discussion over a friendly pint at the pub.

I have taken fifty dollars from petty cash and will ask Simon if he wants to have a drink after work.

Regards, David.

From: David Thorne
Date: Monday 21 November 2011 2.14pm
To: Simon Dempsey
Subject: ndezvous

Dear Simon,

I'm going for a drink after work if you'd care to join me. Your shout.

Regards, David.

....

From: Simon Dempsey
Date: Monday 21 November 2011 2.37pm
To: David Thorne
Subject: Re: ndezvous

No thanks dickhead.

....

From: Jennifer Haines
Date: Monday 21 November 2011 3.56pm
To: Simon Dempsey **CC:** David Thorne
Subject: Appointment with John from TWE

Hello Simon,

Due to Section 3.2 of the Employee Workplace Agreement, when certain accusations are made, the company is required under workplace compliance law to provide reasonable steps to resolve the matter.

As part of this agreement, which you signed, you are required under company policy to complete a government certified course. I have made an appointment with John Bryant from TWE for you to undertake this course at 11.30am next Wednesday.

Additionally, I would appreciate if you and David could discuss and sort out any further issues without resorting to filing out an F26-A as I'm sure all of us have better things to do with our time.

Thank you, Jennifer

....

From: Simon Dempsey
Date: Monday 21 November 2011 4.25pm
To: David Thorne
Subject: No Subject

You fucking liar.

"When I have kids, they won't be allowed to watch television. They can watch the news but that's it. My kids will be highly intelligent and if I let them waste that gift watching Family Guy, what kind of parent would that make me? They should be sculpting or learning the flute instead."

Things Simon has said that annoy me #5

17 reasons not to ask the Internet for advice on puppy names

I have no idea how it happened, I was probably drugged, but we have a puppy in the house. Apparently she is going to with us for the next ninety-odd dog years which is quite a commitment. I was a little concerned about that as the only commitments I generally make are those concerning events at least a week away, which gives me time to think of a way of getting out of them.

I have never lived with a puppy before. When I was young, my sister received a puppy for Christmas but slept with it that night and must have rolled over in her sleep and suffocated it because it was dead the next morning. After many tears, a replacement puppy was found which managed to survive two days; it was playing under an ironing board, pulled the cord, and the iron fell onto its head killing it instantly. The next replacement puppy lasted nearly a week before dying of Parvo, so my sister ended up getting a goldfish. I'm not sure what happened to the goldfish but the bowl was used to house a hermit crab less than a week later, sea-monkeys a few weeks after that, and, eventually, pens.

My first mistake with the new puppy was listening to the advice of other people in regards to buying a 'crate'. "Puppies like the crate," they told me, "it gives them their own space, etc." As it turns out, a crate is a cage. People call it a crate because it is easier to justify keeping a puppy in a crate than a cage. Perhaps, instead of chicken farmers bothering to go to the expense of producing "cage free" eggs, they could just call the cages 'crates' and write on the carton that chickens like crates so that everybody can pretend it isn't something that it is and get cheaper eggs.

I purchased a cage and assembled it on the kitchen floor while the puppy played with the instructions next to me. I then sat looking at both the puppy and the cage for a few minutes before disassembling the cage and putting it out on the sidewalk for the next morning's trash pickup. Then I thought that one of the rubbish truck guys might take it home and use it, so I broke the door off the cage and threw it into a neighbour's hedge.

My second mistake was asking for naming suggestions on the internet. While it was tempting to name the puppy something amusing, this would mean being stuck with a family member named something like Sergeant Chocolate Hat well after the joke wore thin.

Here are just eighteen of the suggestions I received after posting the words "All suggestions welcome" on Twitter and Facebook. I have a suspicion that some of these may have been more aimed at getting me in trouble when I call the puppy's name at the park than actually being helpful:

Emergency Food Supply

Mr. Sassypants

Spinach

Those Things You Put Under Chair Legs To Protect The Carpet

Free Candy

Successful Goiter Surgery

The USS Pogy

Derpington Derp

Grandma

Shaboopy Harris LaGrange III

Battlestar Galactica

Office Secret Santa

Titanic

Professor Gregory Whitesocks

The Thatcher Era

Breakin' 2: Electric Boogaloo

Banana Hammock

Laika

I actually liked the name Laika. Laika was a Soviet space dog that became the first animal to orbit the Earth. She was a stray found on the streets of Moscow. Soviet scientists figured stray animals would be more accustomed to enduring conditions of extreme cold and hunger. To adapt Laika to the confines of the tiny cabin, she was kept in progressively smaller cages for periods up to 20 days. Which she probably liked because I have heard it gives them their own space etc. Before the launch, one of the scientists took Laika home to play with his children, later stating "I wanted to do something nice for her; She had so little time left to live." Which I thought was nice.

Laika was placed in the cockpit of Sputnik 2 and blasted into space on November 3, 1957. After reaching orbit, the rocket's nose cone failed to separate, preventing the thermal control system from operating correctly, which resulted in the cabin temperature rising. Approximately five hours into the flight, no further signs of life were received from the spacecraft. Five months later, after 2,570 orbits of the Earth, Sputnik 2 disintegrated, along with Laika's remains, during re-entry.

So the new puppy is named Laika. It isn't amusing and it doesn't exactly roll off the tongue, but it is a kind of homage and, maybe in some 'dreamcatcher making hippie' way, a part of all the love and attention she receives will somehow find its way back to a scared stray orbiting several hundred kilometres above the earth in her last few moments.

And, yes, I realise that is a bit sentimental but with the addition of another female to the household, making it a three to one ratio, I won't be overly surprised if I start menstruating any day now. Laika has lived with us for only two weeks and I am already more attached than I thought possible. She sleeps on the bed, follows me everywhere, and is spoilt well beyond any sane degree. Stock shares in squeaky toys have probably gone up several points.

Also, for those that told me that without a 'crate' it would take longer to house-train her, while there were a few accidents (which I probably carried on way more about than necessary as I am the kind of person that holds their breath when walking past a dog poo on the street because I read somewhere that if you can smell it, it means you are breathing in fecal mist), it took Laika less than two weeks to learn to scratch at the door when she needs to go out.

Although displaying the ability to learn without the aid of wire, there are, admittedly, some tasks Laika is finding surprisingly difficult. At the age of ten weeks, she still cannot operate the dishwasher and the other day, while working on the car together, I asked her to hand me an adjustable spanner and she brought me a sock. There is no circumstance that I can think of in which a sock would be required for auto maintenance unless maybe tying several socks together, or maybe just a couple of long socks, as a makeshift fan-belt or flag.

Here are a few other simple tasks Laika seems to be having trouble with:

Playing tennis

She has a fairly solid forehand and can slice on her back-swing, but her serve is shocking. In our last match, which resulted in a pretty poor effort of six-zero, six-one, six-zero, I counted a total of thirty-eight double-faults.

Setting ascension and declination

Right ascension is measured eastward along the celestial equator while declination is measured in degrees north or south of the celestial equator. Mixing them up and mistaking the neighbour's yellow bug light on their porch for Saturn means it is someone else's turn to use the telescope and pretend to see things.

Making coffee

There is no excuse for mistakenly selecting a decaf k-cup. Also, there are very few rules in our household but one of them is to fill the Keurig water reservoir for the next person if it is empty. Courtesy is contagious.

Reloading a handgun

It isn't that difficult. A three year old child can do it. I proved this last week while baby-sitting for friends. Until Laika can perform this procedure, she will be of little use in a shoot-out with police or during a zombie apocalypse. Her aim has improved since she stopped anticipating recoil but this counts for little if she is dependent on others to reload her weapon.

Setting depth of field

Yes, the shots of under the couch were nice and the angles are quite creative but there is little point in spending so much on a camera that is permanently set to auto. She may as well use a telephone camera.

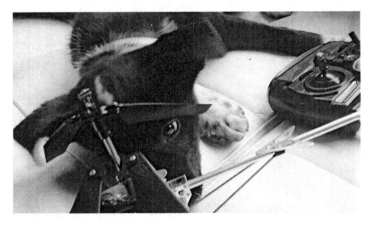

Flying a remote control helicopter

The lever on the left controls elevation, the right, direction. While Laika grasped this fairly quickly, I have had to remind her several times to let go of the levers if the helicopter hits something. Otherwise the propellers will break. They are just plastic and I am not buying a fifth helicopter.

Playing Mortal Kombat

Scorpion's fatality move is forward, up, up, square - not forward, up, square, square. You have to push the up arrow twice. Also, you can't just keep doing the same button sequence to make Scorpion shoot out his spear and say "get over here" every time. You have to mix it up or it isn't fair for the other player. If she keeps doing it, she can play against the computer because it is just wasting my time.

I have taken another thousand or so photos of Laika but I will spare you the task of having to flip through photos of her skateboarding, driving a speedboat, playing chess, and defusing a bomb I made out of cardboard and wires from a broken lamp. There are no photos of Laika in a cage.

Bill tries
to buy cheese
#1

Opinions are like nipples, everybody has one

Despite mentioning cats in only three articles in my previous book, around ninety percent of the emails I receive ask the same two questions; "Did Shannon ever find her missing cat Missy?" and "Why do you hate cats?"

Firstly, yes. Missy was found in a neighbour's hedge that evening. It was about the fifth time she had gone missing and has escaped several times since. Secondly, I don't hate cats. I just don't want them sitting on my lap or rubbing against me lifting their tails so I have to look at their bum holes. If I owned a cat, I would make it wear pants. My partner Holly wants to buy a cat but I have told her that if she gets a cat, I am getting a leather jacket like the one Evel Knievel wore.

Apart from making the occasional joke, which I assume at the time will be taken as such, I would never condone cruelty, violence or tormentation towards any animal. That's what red haired children are for.

From: Ella Johnson
Date: Tuesday 31 May 2011 2.04pm
To: David Thorne
Subject: Book

I've perused your website before and must admit I laughed at the story about the police officer. I work in a bookstore and when your book came in as stock, I made the mistake of browsing through it. While some of it was mildly amusing, you crossed the fine line between dark humour and psychopathy.

It's quite jarring to go from laughing at drawings of spiders to reading your fantasies about torturing and killing cats. This ruined the book for me. Animal cruelty is a mental illness and usually the first sign of a sociopath. Serial killers torture animals when they are young. It's my most fervent opinion that you need to find a highly skilled psychiatrist post-haste and I have left a review on Amazon warning potential buyers.

Ella J

From: David Thorne
Date: Tuesday 31 May 2011 3.28pm
To: Ella Johnson
Subject: Re: Book

Dear Ellla,

Opinions are like nipples, everybody has one. Some have firm points, others are barely discernible through layers, and some are displayed at every opportunity regardless of whether an audience has stated, "I am interested in your nipples" or not. Cats have nineteen.

As people can only provide unbiased opinions about things they have no interest in, your zealous fervour regarding cats is understood but misdirected.

At no time have I ever "fantasized about torturing and killing cats." This is an assumption you have made and I am puzzled to its origin. Are you referring to the article titled David and his best friends spend a day at the beach? I have attached an excerpt.

Regards, David.

From: Ella Johnson
Date: Tuesday 31 May 2011 4.06pm
To: David Thorne
Subject: Re: Re: Book

No of course I'm not because you just made that up. There is nothing in the book about cats making you their king. I was referring to at least 3 articles that mention cats being tortured or killed. The text on the page you mentioned actually states:

"I once agreed to look after a friend's cat for a week but after he dropped it off at my apartment and explained the concept of kitty litter, I kept the cat in a closed cardboard box in the shed and forgot about it. If I wanted to feed something and clean faeces, I wouldn't have put my mother in that home after her stroke. A week later, when my friend came to collect his cat, I pretended that I was not home and mailed the box to him. Apparently I failed to put enough stamps on the package and he had to collect it from the post office and pay eighteen dollars. He still goes on about that sometimes, people need to learn to let go."

The thought of a cat being trapped and frightened in a box in the dark and slowly starving to death is what you call humour? Pathetic. You need to take a good long look at yourself and seriously consider seeing a psychiatrist for your own safety and those around you. I have no idea how you managed to get published by Penguin writing disgusting material that cleary illustrates a complete lack of morals and ethics.

Ella J

....

From: David Thorne
Date: Tuesday 31 May 2011 4.57pm
To: Ella Johnson
Subject: Re: Re: Re: Book

Dear Ella,

I never stated the cat starved to death and you have simply assumed that it didn't enjoy the experience. Cats like being in boxes. Also, it was a fairly big box. I could understand your concern if it had been a shoebox but it was at least twice that size. It is easy to take something written out of its original context and make it look bad; a few years ago, I was commissioned to write copy for an annual publication produced by Top Tourist Parks of Australia. After a print run of seventy-five thousand and distribution throughout Australia and New Zealand, it was discovered that I had left the letter v out of the word 'dive' and the introduction for a family beach resort activity read, "Die with your children. A new world awaits." Apparently a child had drowned the year before so I admit it was bad timing but these things happen, there's no point carrying on about it. Also, despite your opinion that I am without either morals or ethics, many of the articles in the book have an underlying message expressing the contrary. I have attached the article David and his best friends go to the movies, which clearly illustrates this.

Regards, David.

From: Ella Johnson
Date: Wednesday 01 June 2011 9.32am
To: David Thorne
Subject: Re: Re: Re: Re: Book

Obviously we have differing opinions on what constitutes acceptable ethics and offensive humour. I suggest reading some of Chelsea Handler's books. Her humour is spot on and while she can be a bit risque at times, she never crosses the line like your book does. You could learn a lot from her.

Fortunately, in my store at least, I am in a position to dictate where on the shelves your book is displayed so nobody will see it and I will also be sure to warn customers against buying it if they bring it to the counter.

Good luck with sales, you will need it.

Ella J

From: David Thorne
Date: Wednesday 01 June 2011 2.14pm
To: Ella Johnson
Subject: Re: Re: Re: Re: Re: Book

Dear Ella,

Your efforts to protect both cats and customers should not go unacknowledged. If you have access to a printer and scissors, you could make yourself a little badge. Anyone can form an opinion but it takes a certain type of person to carry that opinion through to consumer censorship. In a million years, if mankind dies out and cats inherit the earth, they will probably build a statue of you featuring a cat nestled in one arm, a can of petrol in the other, and a pile of my books at your feet. Or one of you cleaning your bum with your tongue.

Unfortunately, your efforts to impinge book sales are not required as Penguin's marketing team seems to have the same strategy. I visited a Barnes & Noble store this morning, expecting to find copies of my book distributed throughout, but located only a single copy in the home and garden section next to Diana Kennedy's The Art of Mexican Cooking.

I left with a pop-up book about trains and two fridge magnets so I understand the concept of impulse buying, but targeting only those preparing for next year's Cinco de Mayo is a stretch.

In contrast, Chelsea Handler's book was displayed throughout the store and even had its own colourful cardboard display. Based on your suggestion, I had a quick flick through and owe you a debt of gratitude as I now realise what it takes to receive excellent reviews on Amazon from people like yourself.

Regards, David.

From: Ella Johnson
Date: Wednesday 01 June 2011 3.27am
To: David Thorne
Subject: Re: Re: Re: Re: Re: Re: Book

Last email as arguing with a moron is a waste of my valuable time and all you've done is display how ignorant you are. I doubt you've read anything by Chelsea Handler so what would you know. Nobody asked for your opinion anyway.

From: David Thorne
Date: Wednesday 01 June 2011 5.24pm
To: Ella Johnson
Subject: Re: Re: Re: Re: Re: Re: Re: Book

Bill tries
to buy cheese
#2

Ten reasons I probably shouldn't be alive:
humps and bumps

During my last two years of primary school, my family moved from a large city in Western Australia, to a small country town called Leigh Creek, a coal mining town in South Australia. The only two things that were cool about Leigh Creek were the Terex trucks (vehicles the size of buildings) and the fact that almost every kid in town owned a mini-bike.

Every afternoon after school and every weekend, kids would wheel their mini-bikes to the edge of town and ride to a location called *The Humps & Bumps*. It was basically just a series of piles of dirt and quarry k-cuts left over from mining, spanning about a three kilometre radius a few kilometres out of town, but to kids with nothing else to do in a small town, and to those that owned mini-bikes, it was paradise. I did not own a mini-bike and not owning a mini-bike meant exclusion from what was essentially the key to making friends and being accepted in a new town.

The model I coveted was the Yamaha YZ80. Featuring a two stroke engine, knobbly tyres, big suspension for jumps, and a top speed of 55 miles per hour which was practically light speed, it was the mini-bike of all mini-bikes and ownership would instantly grant me acceptance by the Humps & Bumps community.

Convincing my parents to buy me a mini-bike was a lot easier than I thought it would be, possibly due to them feeling guilty about taking me away from my previous school and established friends and moving to a small town, but more likely due to wanting me to shut up about being the only kid in town who didn't own a mini-bike. Eventually, it was conceded that I might get one for my upcoming birthday.

The two weeks leading up to my birthday weekend could not go by fast enough. It was the early eighties and there were no computers, and I had nobody to hang around with as everyone was at the Humps & Bumps, so every afternoon after school I would climb into bed and try to go to sleep to make the time go faster. I even attempted knocking myself out once by sitting on the edge of the bed and throwing a brick into the air, but this only gained me a mild concussion and frozen bag of peas.

On the Saturday morning of my birthday, I leapt out of bed, woke my parents and asked "where's my motorbike?" Told that it was in the backyard, I ran outside in my pajamas to discover my parents had bought me a second hand 50cc Honda postman's scooter.

The stickers that read Australia Post had been peeled off but due to the rest of the paint fading, they were still clearly visible. The front half of the scooter was white, the back half red, and my father had painted DAVID across the back of the huge seat.

I turned to see my parents, wearing dressing gowns and faces of anxious expectancy, standing behind me. My mother stated "Happy birthday. I know it's not a Yamaha like you wanted, but we talked to Mr Williams from number 36 and he said that Honda make very good motorbikes. It used to be a postie's bike so it has to be reliable. Posties need reliable bikes." Although every molecule of my being wanted to yell "what the fuck is this, I can't be seen on it, kids will throw rocks at me," the look on their faces made me force what I hoped was a believable smile, but was probably more of a grimace below two sad eyes, and say, "thank you."

Beaming, my father said, "It's got your name on the seat and you have another present to go with it," handing me a vaguely motorcycle helmet shaped present. Ripping off the paper, which featured a repeated illustration of a guy riding a motorbike that wasn't lame, revealed a construction worker's helmet, probably taken from my fathers worksite, spray-painted black with a skull and crossbones emblazoned across the front. "I painted it myself" my father said, which I had already figured out due to the skull having a smile instead of an angry teeth thing.

After being told "you can take it out for a ride after you get dressed and have breakfast," I spent an hour dressing and another hour eating Froot-Loops by eating each Froot-Loop in the bowl individually and chewing thirty times but eventually the time came to get it over with.

Wheeling the scooter down the sidewalk, wearing the construction worker's helmet and appropriate motorbike attire (shorts, a Battlestar Gallactica t-shirt and sandals), I arrived at the edge of town, started the scooter, and rode off towards an area as far away from the Humps & Bumps as possible.

As I rounded a huge mound of dirt I had intended to hide behind for a while, my heart sank as I saw four kids on mini-bikes riding towards me. Turning the bike around, I attempted to race away from them as quickly as possible, with the thought that my face still hadn't been seen, but with a top speed just under a brisk jog, they caught up to me almost immediately.

Pulling to a stop and as casually as possible saying "Hey," one of the kids, who I recognised as a boy named Ashley from school, asked "Are you delivering the mail?" and the other kids laughed. "No," I replied. Which with hindsight was a little lame and if I could go back I would have said something like "Yes, and I have a letter from your mother. She says she is sorry for giving you a girl's name" or something far better. Another of the kids then stated, "That's a postie's bike. I can see where the stickers were. Is it yours?" and I replied, "No." After a lengthy discussion between the four kids in which every feature of my scooter was analysed and ridiculed, including the fact that it had my name on the seat so it must be mine, I suddenly felt the need to defend the horrible thing and stupidly said "yes, but it's good at jumps."

Riding indian file together to the Humps & Bumps after being told to "prove it then, Postman Pat," we pulled up at the base of a huge hill and the kids pointed to the summit.

The jump was basically a huge track going down the side with a smaller hill at the end acting as a ramp. Riding to the top, I tightened the plastic strap inside my construction hat, and looked down.

Grasping the possibility that there was at least a chance of coming out of this unhurt and earning the acceptance of my peers, I edged forward

Bingo!

and threw back the throttle as hard as I could - snapping the antique piece of tin holding the throttle to the handlebar, and locking it on full. Holding on with every limb tensed like steel, the scooter tore down the incline, hit the ramp at the bottom, and broke in half.

My body, carried by momentum, flipped over the handlebars, cleared the ledge of the ramp, and flew several feet before landing and rolling several times in the dirt. My helmet, which had blown off half way down the hill, rolled to a stop a few feet from me. Dazed, I lay on my back staring up at the sun glimmering through the leaves of a gum tree, listening to the sound of four mini-bikes disappearing at top speed into the distance.

Noticing a throbbing pain in my left leg, I looked down to see my shin bone sticking several inches out of a large gash in my skin, halfway between the knee and ankle. Ignoring earlier advice from my father about getting back on a bike after a fall, I began to drag myself home by sitting up and pulling myself backwards a few feet at a time.

Approximately fifty feet from the crash site, I crawled over an ants' nest and had to roll again, but only twenty minutes later saw the family car driving towards me up the dusty track. Apparently Ashley had ridden to my house and told my parents that despite all four kids trying to convince me otherwise, I had attempted and failed a stunt and broken my scooter. He also visited me in the hospital and, even though he called me Postman Pat for the next two years, we became friends.

My father collected the broken scooter and attempted to repair it by welding the two halves together but it caught on fire and was delegated to the back of the shed never to be seen again.

Which I was quietly happy about. As a token replacement birthday present, I received a Slip'n'Slide which I wasn't allowed to use due to my leg being in a cast but I did get to watch Ashley and his friends using it from my bedroom window.

Also, a week after getting my cast removed, I used the Slip'n'Slide for the first time and, after a large run-up and standing slide that cleared the entire length of the bright yellow plastic, I continued along the grass into a hedge, and a branch punctured my scrotum.

Penguin appreciates your cooperation in this matter.

Since the release of the first book, I am occasionally asked for advice regarding the publishing industry. Which is like asking a five-year-old child to explain Gene Ray's Timecube theory. I generally just wing it and see what happens; regardless of the outcome, it is usually at least interesting and there is far too much wank involved to take it seriously.

Distribution and royalty issues with my first publisher left me with the impression that their company consisted entirely of a fifteen-year-old kid working from his parent's shed. Working with my second publisher, Penguin, was a lengthy but, for the most part, enjoyable process. The decision not to publish this second book with Penguin was based on timing, not on any dissatisfaction. Working with a large publisher like Penguin has benefits, such as a marketing budget, but the process from initial contract to release of royalties is very slow. When this book was first released, the cover featured a penguin giving the finger (page 111). It ambiguously made sense with the title, was cute, and... I had no marketing budget. While it is important to pick your battles and I have no intention of facing Penguin's army of lawyers in a courtroom that I would probably need to borrow the airfare to get to, I figured there was a good likelihood of Penguin sending me a cease and desist letter. Which is publicity you can't buy and even if you could, I couldn't because I don't have any money.

From: Donald Snadek
Date: Wednesday 14 March 2012 3.23pm
To: David Thorne
Subject: Trademark Infringement

Dear Mr. Thorne:

Your use of our Penguin mark on the book's cover and your website is an infringement of our trademark. Our parent company, Pearson plc, and our affiliate, Penguin Books Limited, which is the registered owner of the mark, demand that we strictly enforce our trademark rights.

We therefore must insist that you immediately remove all images of the book's cover from the Internet, and that you also immediately cease selling copies of the book with that cover.

Please confirm in writing that you will take the required steps by no later than Friday, March 16, 2012. This is not an idle threat. If you don't comply, we will take legal action against you, which will include seeking recovery of our attorneys' fees.

Donald K. Snadek

....

From: David Thorne
Date: Thursday 15 March 2012 10.18am
To: Donald Snadek
Subject: Re: Trademark Infringement

Dear Donald,

I have received your email in regards to the infringement of Penguin's trademark. The image was chosen as it related to the arctic environment implied in the title and not meant to imply any umbrage with Penguin or penguins as a whole.

Am I to understand that despite using the same image of a penguin giving the finger (which has at least a thirty degree difference in the angle of the flipper to Penguin's logo) to promote the first book without any issue, now that I am using it to promote the second book, which is not published by Penguin, it is a trademark infringement?

Regards, David.

Lucius as a beautiful unicorn

VON MALTITZ, DERENBERG, KUNIN, JANSSEN & GIORDANO

▉▉▉▉▉ STREET
NEW YORK, N. Y. 10165

TELEPHONE (▉▉▉▉▉▉▉▉▉)
FAX (212)▉▉▉▉▉

<u>VIA EMAIL AND FEDERAL EXPRESS</u>

March 23, 2012

David Thorne
▉▉▉▉▉▉▉▉▉▉▉▉▉▉▉▉▉▉

Dear Mr. Thorne:

We write on behalf of our clients, Penguin Books Limited, a UK company, and its U.S. affiliate Penguin Group (USA) Inc., to object to your unauthorized use of a close imitation of our clients' famous penguin design mark on the cover and title page of your recent book, <u>I'll Go Home Then, It's Warm and Has Chairs. The Unpublished Emails</u>, and on your web site. These uses infringe, dilute, and tarnish our clients' mark.

Penguin Books Limited is the owner of the famous trademarks "PENGUIN" and a representation of a penguin. For many decades, our client and its predecessors have extensively used their PENGUIN word and design marks, as well as the trade name "Penguin," throughout the United States and abroad. As you know, our clients' PENGUIN marks and trade name are among the best known in the publishing field. The good will they symbolize is inestimable, and our clients are firmly committed to protecting their integrity.

Penguin Books Limited owns the following federal trademark registrations, among others:

Representation of Penguin, No. 557,412 of April 8, 1952 for books;

Representation of Penguin in Orange Oval No. 2,666,054 of Dec. 24, 2002 for "house mark for a full line of fiction and non-fiction books covering a variety of subjects"; and

PENGUIN, No. 561,636 of July 15, 1952 for books.

Copies of these registrations are enclosed as Exhibits A-C. These registrations are incontestable and thus, under the U.S. Trademark Act, constitute conclusive evidence of our clients' exclusive right to use the registered marks.

VON MALTITZ, DERENBERG, KUNIN, JANSSEN & GIORDANO

David Thorne   March 23, 2012

      The penguin logo prominently displayed on the front cover and title page of your recent book, and on your web site, closely simulates our clients' famous penguin design mark and will inevitably cause confusion. It is displayed not only on your book's front cover and title page but also, in the image of the book on your web site, on the book's spine, where our clients' penguin design and other publishers' colophons regularly appear. And it is displayed against an orange background similar to the orange widely used by our clients on their books and web sites.

      Furthermore, because Penguin is the publisher of your first book (a fact publicized in your recent book and on your web site), the public is especially likely to believe your recent book, prominently displaying a penguin logo, is also published by Penguin. Your web site further encourages this mistake by displaying your infringing penguin logo next to the announcement that "The second book is out now." (Exhibit D).

      The U.S. Trademark Act defines infringement as the use, without the trademark owner's consent, of "any reproduction, counterfeit, copy, or colorable imitation of a registered mark in connection with the sale, offering for sale, distribution, or advertising of any goods or services on or in connection with which such use is likely to cause confusion, or to cause mistake, or to deceive." [15 U.S. Code 1114(1)(a)] . The state laws of unfair competition are essentially the same.

      Your unauthorized penguin logo therefore infringes our client's federally registered Penguin design mark and also constitutes unfair competition under U.S. federal and state laws.

      Furthermore, your depiction of our client's penguin design mark making a vulgar gesture wrongfully tarnishes it and dilutes its distinctiveness in violation of the U.S. Federal Anti-Dilution Act [15 USC 1125(c)] and the dilution laws of many U.S. states. Such wrongful dilution may occur even when there is no likelihood of confusion.

      The excuses offered in your March 15, 2012 email to ████████████ are legally without merit:

      (1) "I'm not using the trademark logo, it is also more than 30% different"

      There is no "30% different" defense to trademark infringement or dilution. As mentioned above, under the U.S. Trademark Act colorable imitations as well as counterfeits are infringements. The penguin logo on your book and web site is a very close imitation.

Courts have often found confusing similarity and infringement where the parties' marks were less alike than they are here. For example, in <u>Mutual of Omaha Ins. Co. v. Novak</u>, 836 F.2d 397, 402 (8th Cir.1987), the defendant changed "Mutual of Omaha" to "Mutant of Omaha" and also modified the plaintiff's Indian head logo. The court found the resulting mark "confusing."

While there are differences that can be pointed out in a side-by-side comparison, on the whole the name and logo created a substantially similar concept, image and feel which the Court finds is likely to create confusion as to source, affiliation or sponsorship on the part of consumers.

Similarly, making changes to a famous mark is not enough to escape liability for dilution. <u>Starbucks Corp. v. Wolfe's Borough Coffee, Inc.</u>, 588 F.3d 97 (2nd Cir. 2009) (no requirement of substantial similarity to the diluted mark). To the contrary, where, as here, the changes add negative features, they increase the likelihood of dilution liability. <u>Deere & Co. v. MTD Products, Inc.</u>, 41 F.3d 39 (2d Cir. 1994). As discussed below, your vulgar variation of our clients' design mark tarnishes it and is thus a separate statutory wrongful dilution. [15 USC § 1125(c)(1)].

(2) <u>The penguin logo is "used under parody."</u>

As stated by a leading trademark commentator, "[T]he cry of 'parody!' does not magically fend off otherwise legitimate claims of trademark infringement or dilution." <u>6 McCarthy on Trademarks and Unfair Competition</u> § 31:153 (4th ed.).

Your recent book is a collection of pieces on various subjects unrelated to our clients. The vulgar simulation of our clients' mark on your book's cover is not for the purpose of parody but to draw attention to your book and trade on the mark's fame and good will. Your claim of "use under parody" is therefore baseless. <u>McCarthy</u>, § 31:153. Parody claims more plausible than yours have repeatedly been rejected by the courts when there was no parodic justification for the use of the plaintiff's mark. E.g., <u>Elvis Presley Enterprises, Inc. v. Capece</u>, 141 F.3d 188 (5th Cir. 1998) (defendants' use of tavern name "The Velvet Elvis" as part of an alleged parody of "a time or concept from the sixties—the Las Vegas lounge scene, the velvet painting craze and perhaps indirectly, the country's fascination with Elvis" does not justify the use of Elvis' name).

Furthermore, even if your recent book were a parody, this would not be a defense where, as here, there is a likelihood of confusion. <u>Presley Enterprises, Inc. v. Capece</u>, 141 F.3d 188 (5th Cir. 1998) (parody not a defense to infringement but only a factor that may be considered in determining whether confusion is likely).

David Thorne   March 23, 2012

Parody is also not a defense to your tarnishment of our clients' penguin design mark by displaying it making a vulgar gesture. E.g., Coca-Cola Co. v. Gemini Rising, Inc., 346 F. Supp. 1183 (EDNY 1972) (rejecting a parody defense by a seller of posters displaying ENJOY COCAINE in the same script and red and white colors used by Coca-Cola); Anheuser-Busch, Inc. v Andy's Sportswear, Inc., 40 U.S.P.Q.2d 1542 (N.D. Cal. 1996) (BUDWEISER trademark owner granted temporary restraining order against use of BUTTWISER on T-shirts).

In short, your attempted parody excuse fails because "the parody has to be a takeoff, not a ripoff." Nike, Inc. v. "Just Did It" Enterprises, 6 F.3d 1225, 1228 (7th Cir.1993).

Our clients regard your infringing penguin logo as a serious violation of their trademark rights and will not tolerate it. We demand that:

(1) you immediately cease selling the book with the infringing cover and title page and permanently refrain from using any other confusingly similar penguin word or design mark,

(2) by March 30, 2012, you (a) permanently remove the infringing penguin logo from your web site and from all other promotional or advertising materials or web sites subject to your control, (b) notify all on-line and brick-and-mortar sellers to remove the book from sale, and (c) instruct all on-line sellers to take down the infringing penguin logo, and

(3) by April 2, 2012, you provide us with written confirmation that you have taken all the steps demanded.

If you fail to comply with these demands, our clients will take legal action against you under the U.S. Trademark Act for willful infringement. In addition to an injunction, a court may award our clients (1) your profits from the infringement, (2) up to three times our clients' damages, (3) our clients' reasonable attorneys' fees, and (4) the other costs of the litigation. [U.S. Trademark Act, Section 35 (15 USC § 1117)].

We await your response acknowledging that you will comply in full with our clients' demands.

Very truly yours,

Encs.

Int. Cl.: 16

Prior U.S. Cl.: 38

United States Patent and Trademark Office

10 Year Renewal

Reg. No. 557,412
Registered Apr. 8, 1952
Renewal Term Begins Apr. 8, 1992

TRADEMARK
PRINCIPAL REGISTER

PENGUIN BOOKS LIMITED (ENGLAND COMPANY)
BATH ROAD, HARMONDSWORTH MIDDLESEX, ENGLAND UB7 0DA, BY MESNE ASSIGNMENT FROM PENGUIN BOOKS, INC. (MARYLAND CORPORATION) BALTIMORE, MD

FOR: BOOKS, IN CLASS 38 (INT. CL. 16).

FIRST USE 0-0-1940; IN COMMERCE 0-0-1940.

SER. NO. 71-615,020, FILED 6-11-1951.

In testimony whereof I have hereunto set my hand and caused the seal of The Patent and Trademark Office to be affixed on June 2, 1992.

COMMISSIONER OF PATENTS AND TRADEMARKS

EXHIBIT A

Int. Cl.: 16

Prior U.S. Cls.: 2, 5, 22, 23, 29, 37, 38 and 50

United States Patent and Trademark Office

Amended

Reg. No. 2,666,054

Registered Dec. 24, 2002

OG Date Apr. 17, 2007

TRADEMARK
PRINCIPAL REGISTER

PENGUIN BOOKS LIMITED (UNITED
KINGDOM CORPORATION)
BATH ROAD
HARMONDSWORTH
MIDDLESEX, ENGLAND UB7 0DA
OWNER OF U.S. REG. NOS. 537,412,
2,034,691 AND OTHERS.
COLOR IS CLAIMED AS A FEATURE
OF THE MARK.
THE MARK CONSISTS OF A PEN-
GUIN, COLORED BLACK AND WHITE,
DISPLAYED WITHIN AN ORANGE
OVAL.

FOR: HOUSE MARK FOR A FULL
LINE OF FICTION AND NONFICTION
BOOKS COVERING A VARIETY OF
SUBJECTS, IN CLASS 16 (U.S. CLS. 2, 5,
22, 23, 29, 37, 38 AND 50).

FIRST USE 6-0-1936, THE MARK WAS
FIRST USED ANYWHERE IN A
DIFFERENT FORM OTHER THAN THAT
SOUGHT TO BE REGISTERED ON
00/00/1940; IN COMMERCE 0-0-1936.

SER. NO. 76-333,017, FILED 11-2-2001.

*In testimony whereof I have hereunto set my hand
and caused the seal of The Patent and Trademark
Office to be affixed on Apr. 17, 2007.*

DIRECTOR OF THE U.S. PATENT AND TRADEMARK OFFICE

EXHIBIT B

EXHIBIT C

From: David Thorne
Date: Wednesday 28 March 2012 2.14pm
To: Donald Snadek
Subject: The big letter

Dear Donald,

I have received your letter and, as I could probably list ten thousand things that would be more fun than facing Penguin in court (starting with 1. making long lists) for what was essentially a joke that related to the cold environment implied in the title, I will immediately capitulate to your demands.

Regards, David.

....

From: Donald Snadek
Date: Wednesday 28 March 2012 4.52pm
To: David Thorne
Subject: Re: The big letter

Dear Mr. Thorne:

Thank you for your message. Penguin appreciates your cooperation in this matter.

To avoid any misunderstanding, however, I want to remind you that our March 23 letter demanded not only a change in your book's cover but also of all materials on which the infringing logo appears. This includes the book's title page and promotional materials, such as the T-shirts and mugs displayed on your web site and offered on online stores. It also includes not only your web site but also any display of or link to the infringing logo on your Facebook, Twitter or other personal social network pages.

Our March 23 letter demanded that these sites be changed by March 30. Please confirm that you understand this.

Donald K. Snadek

From: David Thorne
Date: Thursday 29 March 2012 10.21am
To: Donald Snadek
Subject: Re: Re: The big letter

Dear Donald,

Yes, the version of the letter I received was predominately in English. Even with my reading disability (my bedside lamp is only 25w) and skipping to the pictures after page two due to its length, I was able to understand the gist; "We are angryface and would like you to use a picture of a cat or something instead of a penguin."

Regards, David.

From: Donald Snadek
Date: Thursday 29 March 2012 12.04pm
To: David Thorne
Subject: Re: Re: Re: The big letter

Yes, a cat instead of a penguin would be acceptable.

From: David Thorne
Date: Thursday 29 March 2012 12.17pm
To: Donald Snadek
Subject: Re: Re: Re: Re: The big letter

What if a penguin is riding the cat? Perhaps in a race.

From: Donald Snadek
Date: Thursday 29 March 2012 3.19pm
To: David Thorne
Subject: Re: Re: Re: Re: Re: The big letter

That would not be acceptable.

From: Donald Snadek
Date: Tuesday 3 April 2012 11.32am
To: David Thorne
Subject: Penguin trademark

Dear Mr. Thorne:

In your March 29 email, you stated that you "understood the gist" of our March 28 email: namely, that your infringing penguin logo was to be changed no later than March 30. As of today, four days beyond the deadline, your book now features a penguin holding flowers, despite your email stating that you would change the penguin to a cat.

We demand, no later than the close of business on April 4, that you comply with our demands. If not, Penguin will seek injunctive relief and damages. You will not receive further warning before Penguin takes legal action.

Donald K. Snadek

....

From: David Thorne
Date: Tuesday 3 April 2012 12.54pm
To: Donald Snadek
Subject: Re: Penguin trademark

Dear Donald,

As I understood from your letter, your main concerns were that the penguin cover was **a.** making a rude gesture, **b.** presented on an orange background, and **c.** recognisable as the Penguin logo and the association with Penguin that brings. The redesigned penguin is now **a.** making a kind gesture, **b.** presented on a background devoid of any colour, **c.** with a quick glance, perhaps in a room lit by a 25w light globe, could be more immediately mistaken for the work of a shy British vandal than the Penguin logo in question, and **d.** not racing a cat.

Surely Penguin does not claim ownership to all penguin related imagery. If so, are you intending to send the same email to Linux, McVitie's, Otmar Guttman, and Amundsen-Scott Station?

Regards, David.

From: Donald Snadek
Date: Wednesday 4 April 2012 11.06am
To: David Thorne
Subject: Re: Re: Penguin trademark

Dear Mr. Thorne:

As stated in our most recent email, your current penguin logo (holding flowers) is not acceptable. The test of infringement is not whether your logo is identical to Penguin's logo or even whether your logo is likely to be mistaken for Penguin's logo. The test is whether your logo sufficiently resembles Penguin's logo to cause confusion about the relationship of your book to Penguin. Your use of a penguin logo is likely to cause members of the public to believe that Penguin publishes your second as well as your first book, and that Penguin has designed or authorized this variation of its usual Penguin logo. We already have evidence that such confusion has occurred. Furthermore, trademark law has a "safe distance" rule that someone who has previously infringed (as you have) must stay further away from the plaintiff's trademark than one who has not previously infringed.

For these reasons, we repeat our demand that, by the close of business tomorrow, you permanently change the design of your logo to something that is not a penguin.

Donald K. Snadek

From: David Thorne
Date: Wednesday 4 April 2012 1.47pm
To: Donald Snadek
Subject: Re: Re: Re: Penguin trademark

Dear Donald,

Understood. Can you please check with Penguin if something along the lines of the attached would be acceptable to them.

The sticker flash thing hides the fact that it is a penguin, with the word 'cat' included to convince those suspicious that it may be a penguin otherwise. This solves both Penguin's issue with the book cover and my issue with having to do anything that requires actual effort.

I look forward to hearing from you at your convenience and hope we can put this matter to a close.

Regards, David.

NOW WITH A STICKER COVERING THE PICTURE OF A CAT THROWING FLOWERS!

From: Donald Snadek
Date: Thursday 5 April 2012 10.04am
To: David Thorne
Subject: Re: Re: Re: Re: Penguin trademark

Dear Mr. Thorne:

This matter will come to a close only when you comply to our demands. Your proposed "cat" is instantly recognizable as a penguin by anyone who has seen your current or original penguin cover, and by anyone else who knows that black and white "cats" do not have webbed feet.

This is my last correspondence with you before we proceed with legal action. I strongly suggest you change the image immediately. Your book does not contain any articles about penguins but many about cats. I understand the title suggests a cold environment but there are any number of alternatives to Antarctica such as skiing or being in space.

Donald K. Snadek

Ten reasons I probably shouldn't be alive:
Being stabbed

There is an old saying that you can choose your friends but not your relatives. Or something like that. If this was true, I would be friends with Brad Pitt and he would buy me lots of presents and take me shopping. Probably for expensive watches and boats that have lounge chairs in the back.

I have been asked a few times what being stabbed felt like and the only way I can describe it is that it was like a sharp stabbing pain. If you were expecting an appropriate simile or six paragraph description, you should probably have bought a book by Emily Brontë instead. I read a book by Brontë once. She went on for about two hundred pages about a cup of tea. I'm sure it was a great cup of tea but if you can't describe a cup of tea in one sentence, there are a lot of other books out there that can get to a point. A point that hopefully has something to do with robots. I stopped reading before the kettle boiled but I'm sure it all turned out fine.

There is usually some form of bond between relatives, but I never felt it with one named Christopher. I didn't have a lot to do with him as a kid and while family gatherings demanded some small interaction, for the most part we kept to ourselves. My interests centred mainly around reading and drawing while Christopher's one fixation was the World Wrestling Federation. His bedroom walls were covered with posters of some guy wearing a kilt named Rowdy Roddy Piper. The one above his bed had the words 'Hot Rod' emblazoned across it in a lightning shaped typeface.

He was a little slow but not in the Forrest Gump kind of way, more the 'patiently explaining instructions twice before doing it yourself' kind of way. It was a common rumour that he wore a nappy until the age of eight but I have always suspected this was due more to laziness than anything else as he was a fairly fat kid. After I left home to attend University, I didn't really have much to do with him. He lived at home until his late thirties so I would, on occasion, catch up with him at family events but as his interests only expanded enough from wrestling to include pornography, we did not have a lot to chat about. Mentioning anything about art and design was met with statements such as "designers are poofters unless they are the kind who design custom graphics for Harley Davidsons" and "I've got tons of naked chicks on my computer, that's all the art I need."

Somewhere along the line, Christopher gained 300 pounds in body mass and a girlfriend named Joylene of similar dimension. I visited the flat they rented together once but twenty minutes of sitting on a dog's beanbag within touching distance of a kitty litter tray that hadn't been changed in months while watching the movie White Chicks was pretty much it for me.

While far from having OCD, I prefer things un-messy which is why I keep everything I own in clearly labelled boxes. I currently have over four thousand boxes of various shapes and sizes. I keep the smaller boxes in larger boxes clearly marked 'smaller boxes'.

I can't recall what excuse I gave to leave but I'm fairly sure it was more polite than "Your dog is eating poo from the kitty litter and no, helping you install a stolen Audio4 stereo in your car after the movie does not sound... fuck this, I'm going." Before I left, Chris used my phone to order pizza because his was out of credit and, as I was leaving, asked for pizza money and didn't have change for a fifty.

I only heard from Christopher three times in the years following. Once to decline helping him torch his Ford Falcon on a quiet country road in the middle of the night to claim the insurance money, once to store a wooden boat in my shed, and once when he needed somewhere to stay due to Joylene discovering several terrabytes of teen art on his computer. After living alone for several years, I was hesitant to let anyone stay in my apartment, let alone Christopher, but after being assured it would only be "for a few days at the most," I reluctantly agreed.

Hey. How you doing?

Six weeks later, returning home from work early one afternoon, I walked into my kitchen to discover Christopher dressed in women's lingerie and a curly blonde wig, mounted on the handle of a toilet plunger suctioned securely to the floor. He looked like a huge albino frog lollipop. A K-Mart brochure lay open between his knees advertising children's swimwear.

As Christoper leapt up in surprise, the plunger handle exited and, like a trebuchet, flung a combination of butter and faeces across the kitchen cabinets. My first reaction was to stand there in shock. Christopher's first reaction was to grab a Wiltshire® steak knife from the kitchen counter top and plunge it four inches into my stomach. He then ran up the stairs as I slid slowly down the refrigerator door to the floor.

I have no problem with anyone's sexual preferences. I read about a man once who married a cabbage so, by comparison, most people's preferences are fairly tame. When I was about eight, I laid on the bathroom floor and cracked an egg onto my penis, I have no idea why, and if I thought it would feel even remotely nice, I would probably stick things in my bottom as well. It's good to have a hobby. I'd probably start on something small, like someone else's toothbrush, and work my way up to watermelons or something. I wouldn't do it while staying at someone else's house though.

Descending a few minutes later, with his bags hurriedly packed, Christopher said "That will teach you not to give away people's boats" and left. On the way out, he stole my wallet from the hallway table and scratched a deep groove down the side of my car with a key. For some reason, I will put it down to shock, I edged my way up from the floor, with the knife handle still protruding from my abdomen, made it into the lounge area and watched a re-run of MASH. It was the episode where Klinger tried to eat a Jeep. Attempting several times to slowly remove the serrated blade, and almost blacking out from the pain each time, I decided to drive to the hospital.

I was approximately two blocks from the hospital when a police car pulled me over for not wearing my seatbelt. Explaining to the officer that I was unable to secure the seatbelt due to the knife handle protruding from my stomach and stating "No, I don't need an ambulance, the hospital is just around the corner," I had my keys taken from me and was forced to wait almost an hour for an ambulance to arrive.

While we were waiting, the officer asked me what had happened and I told him that I had slipped on butter on the kitchen floor and fell onto the open dishwasher door which had a steak knife facing up in the thing that holds cutlery. I have no idea why I made up this story as I certainly felt no need to protect Chris but part of my brain seems hardwired to always automatically lie to police and at the time it seemed a more viable scenario than the truth. 'Kitchen accident' was listed on the hospital report and I was in surgery for less than hour, receiving only five stitches. Apparently the knife had missed my lung by two centimetres and no major organs had been damaged.

Returning home later that night, I cleaned both the kitchen and the room Chris had been staying in and found my son's Star Wars® lightsabre, the missing rubber duck from the bathroom, and a pair of size 20 women's blue satin panties under the bed, coated in the same concoction as the plunger.

Not knowing what other items had been included in Christopher's activities meant I had to throw out everything in the house that could theoretically fit inside a human bottom. I told my son that I'd given all his toys to a poor family and had to take him to Toys'R'Us to buy replacements.

Sexy Centrefold

Name
Simon Dempsey

Starsign
Gamera the flying turtle

Turn ons
Nickelback, Whoopi Goldberg, room temperature, pushing buttons with a smooth push button action, and getting a little bit wet in the rain then quickly running inside.

Turn offs
Amazon shipping delays

Fondest Childhood Memory
The day I woke up and my nipples were completely gone. No scars or anything, just flat skin. When I left my room, I found out my dad had died the previous night and that for my entire life, he had been sneaking into my room while I slept and sucking on my chest to make two giant hickeys where my nipples should have been because I was born without them. Not for any sexual reason, just so I would fit in.

Favourite Sexual Position
The shopping trolley. It's where you look at porn while your partner is out buying groceries.

Favourite Quote
"Two thumbs up" The Daily Review.

David and his best friends go for a drive

You have to do your timesheets. Everyone does.

I don't like doing time-sheets. I mentioned this to Holly and she said "God you are lazy, just write down when you arrive and leave. How hard can it be?" Which must apparently be how it works in non-design related companies. Although designers are rarely known for their organisational skills, we are expected to compile a methodical record throughout the day of each project we are working on. I generally refuse to do this. Partly because there would be far too many unaccountable hours to explain and partly because if I wanted to 'clock in, clock off,' I would work in a factory. Probably making garage-door remotes or something. Even then, I doubt I would be expected to write down 'Made a garage-door remote' after making each garage-door remote.

I once tried to implement an office procedure where, at 4.30pm each day, everyone would insult each other for fifteen minutes and then, for the last fifteen minutes of each day, apologise to each person for what had been said. This way, everyone would leave happy with all issues sorted. It did not go down well. Two formal complaints were made and the secretary locked herself in the toilet and cried.

Also, I received a bit of flack after posting a series of formal complaints recently. They are included in this book. Apparently, I was picking on Simon for no other reason than to be cruel and tormentive. While I am happy to be labeled such, there are many other reasons to pick on Simon. Here are just three:

1. Simon super-glued his calculator to his desk to stop people borrowing it. Its position at the back of the desk and the angle of the LCD screen requires that he stand to use it.

2. Simon times and records toilet breaks and personal calls on his time-sheets. He also times and records the time it takes him to do his time-sheets on his time-sheets.

3. I once asked Simon what three items he would rescue from a house fire and he replied, "My cat, the home insurance policy, and my Invicta watch collection."

From: Simon Dempsey
Date: Monday 13 February 2012 9.11am
To: David Thorne
Subject: Timesheets

Did you use my desk while I was away? You're not allowed to go on my computer. I can tell someone used it because I shut it down before I left and pulled out the power cord but it was on this morning and where is my mousepad and what is this shit drawn on my desk?

I need to collect everyones time sheets for last week as well. Have you done them?

....

From: David Thorne
Date: Monday 13 February 2012 9.52am
To: Simon Dempsey
Subject: Re: Timesheets

Good morning Simon,

No, I have decided not to do time-sheets anymore. I'm not a robot. As your new token responsibility as time-sheet collector is essentially the office equivalent of placing an OCD child in charge of equally spaced fridge-magnet distribution to keep it occupied while The View is on, this saves you from having to bother with the whole embarrassing process.

Also, while I generally avoid going anywhere near your cubicle of sorrow, lest the lack of atmosphere suck me in and cause my eyes to pop out like in that Arnold Schwarzenegger movie where he is on Mars and his eyes pop out, I was required to access your computer in your absence due to a client's request for files.

I actually missed you while you were away. To counter this, I placed a plank of wood in your chair and wrote 'Simon' on it. He said I could use your stuff.

Regards, David.

Attached image: Foyer.jpg

Margin note:

Occasionally, I watch my coworkers going about their daily duties and wonder what they think and what they do after hours when they get home. Most of the time though, I couldn't give a fuck.

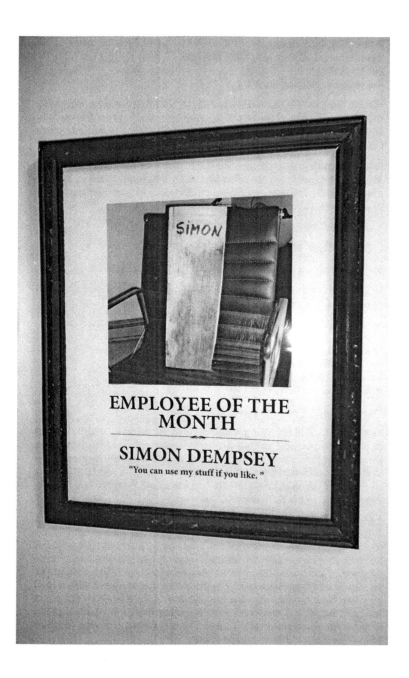

From: Simon Dempsey
Date: Monday 13 February 2012 10.05am
To: David Thorne
Subject: Re: Re: Timesheets

YOURE NOT ALLOWED TO USE MY COMPUTER. What client needed a file off my computer? Youre not allowed to put things on the walls in the foyer either. It leaves holes. It was a waste of time anyway because I took it straight down. Some of us have work to do you know.

And you don't just get to choose if you do your time sheets or not . You're not special. Its the rules and accounts need them to bill the client properly. I've been here longer than you and I put my time sheets in every week. Everyone has to do them.

1. YOURE NOT ALLOWED NOT TOUCH MY COMPUTER

2. DO NOT USE MY STUFF

3. YOU HAVE TO DO YOUR TIMESHEETS. EVERYONE DOES.

I took a photo of my desk and am going to email it to Jennifer. Is it permanent marker? And where are my pens dickhead?

....

From: David Thorne
Date: Monday 13 February 2012 11.08am
To: Simon Dempsey
Subject: Re: Re: Re: Timesheets

Dear Simon,

I understand that following a set of rules saves you from having to make decisions but, as you are well aware, all branding services provided by this company are charged at a fixed quote and price. As such, time spent doing time-sheets might be better spent questioning the logic of requiring time-sheets to calculate a fee that has already been agreed upon. Or cleaning your desk.

I once read about five monkeys that were placed in a room with a banana at the top of a set of stairs. As one monkey attempted to climb the stairs, all of the monkeys were sprayed with jets of cold water. A second monkey made an attempt and again the monkeys were sprayed. No more monkeys attempted to climb the stairs. One of the monkeys was then removed from the room and replaced with a new monkey. New monkey saw the banana and started to climb the stairs but to its surprise, it was attacked by the other monkeys. Another of the original monkeys was replaced and the newcomer was also attacked when he attempted to climb the stairs.

The previous newcomer took part in the punishment with enthusiasm. Replacing a third original monkey with a new one, it headed for the stairs and was attacked as well. Half of the monkeys that attacked him had no idea why. After replacing the fourth and fifth original monkeys, none had ever been sprayed with cold water but all stayed the fuck away from the stairs.

Being here longer than me doesn't automatically make your adherence to a rule, or the rule itself, right. It makes you the fifth replacement monkey. The one with the weird red arse and the first to point and screech when anyone approaches the stairs. I would be the sixth monkey, at home in bed trying to come up with a viable excuse not to spend another fruitless day locked in a room with five neurotic monkeys.

Regardless, you will be pleased to learn that due to your absence last week leaving me with a spare hour per day, which is usually dedicated to staring at the back of your head with one eye closed doing that thing with your thumb and finger where you squash it, I did do my time-sheets.

Please find attached.

Regards, David.

MONDAY

9am
Arrived at work. Considered staying home in bed but, with Simon being away this week, there is no real reason to be absent. Checked production schedule. Completed my work for the week.

4pm
Cleaned my mouse.

5pm
Left for the day.

TUESDAY

10am
Arrived at work. Answered the phone on Simon's desk with "Hello, this is Simon Dempsey speaking. How may I be of help to you?" Told client I would have a pdf to them "as quick as a cheetah."

10.30am
Accessed Simon's computer using his secret password 'Archmage' in

order to locate and send requested pdf to client. Sent.

Read Simon's emails. Replied to his mother regarding her question about what to get Auntie Maureen for her birthday. Recommended jumping castle.

11.30am
Attempted to log into Simon's Facebook. Clicked 'send me my password.' Checked Simon's email. Logged into Simon's Facebook.

Changed status to single. Sent Karen a message saying "Ignore the status change. We haven't broken up. I just don't want anyone to know I have a girlfriend."

Looked at pictures Simon uploaded of himself in a boat. Googled the names of the two guys in Miami Vice. Tagged Simon's nipples 'Sony' and 'Chubbs'.

4pm
Left for the day.

WEDNESDAY

11.am
Arrived at work. Read about Emperor penguins on Wikipedia while having my morning coffee at Simon's desk. Drew pictures of penguins.

11.30am
Realised the permanent Sharpie I was drawing with had penetrated the paper and Simon's desk now had eighteen penguins saying 'Hey' on it.

Hunting for something to clean it with, I used the key Simon hides behind the framed photo of his cat Lady Diana to unlock his top drawer. Found Star Wars Lego.

Recreated the scene from the movie where, during a light-saber duel, Vader cuts off Luke's right hand, reveals that he is his father, and entreats him to convert to the dark side so they can rule the galaxy as father and son. Lost Luke's hand behind Simon's desk.

12.30pm
Chased and killed a bee in the office with Simon's mousepad rolled into a tube while making light-saber noises. Closed Simon's window.

12.45pm
Thought about the bee's family waiting expectantly at home for his return. Gave them names. Imagined Bradley rushing into his mother's outstretched arms, bewailing, "I miss him so much" and Brenda replying, "I know Bradley, I miss him too."

Performed ceremony. There was cake. Constructed a small funereal pyre on Simon's desk out of a paperclip, placed Ben's small lifeless body on top, mentioned his selfless determination to provide for his family, and set it alight.

Unfortunately, I was only into the first verse of Bohemian Rhapsody, the only church song I know, when Ben's body popped like a corn kernel and flew behind the desk. Unsure if he was still alight, I poured coffee down after him.

Realising nobody has ever been behind Simon's desk due to its size and position against a rear wall, I also dropped the remains of the cake and the plate down the back to save me having to walk into the kitchen. Accidently knocked Simon's pencils down there as well. And then his mousepad.

3pm
Left for the day.

THURSDAY

12pm
Arrived at work.

1pm
Sat in Simon's chair without my pants on.

2pm
Left for the day.

FRIDAY

Called in sick. Went shopping. Bought a Keurig.

....

From: Simon Dempsey
Date: Monday 13 February 2012 11.29am
To: David Thorne
Subject: Re: Re: Re: Re: Timesheets

Thanks for the evidence dickhead. I emailed that to Jennifer and i changed my password. I am making a formal complaint. Stay off my computer or I will punch you in the throat. I am serious. Are you going to get my stuff out from behind the desk?

....

From: David Thorne
Date: Monday 13 February 2012 11.41am
To: Simon Dempsey
Subject: Re: Re: Re: Re: Re: Timesheets

Dear Simon,

I wish I had the time. Some of us have work to do and time sheets to complete. I have attached today's should you wish to also email to Jennifer.

Regards, David.

"Did you know that if you multiply 1089 x 9 you get 9801. It's reversed itself! It also works with 10989 or 109989 or 1099989 and so on."

Things Simon has said that annoy me #8

MONDAY

9am

Arrived at work. I feel it is important to set a good example for the other staff through promptness.

9.11am

Received a series of rather vicious emails from Simon, which began with accusations, insults, questions and demands, and degraded into actual threats of bodily harm. This was after I told him I had missed him while he was away. I find this unprovoked animosity disappointing and would have expected more from the employee of the month.

11.30am

Filled out these time sheets as it is part of the job and allows production to bill the client accordingly. Finding it difficult to concentrate on job priorities today due to the negative environment Simon has created, so will be leaving at lunch time.who will get in trouble dickhead.

....

From: Simon Dempsey
Date: Monday 13 February 2012 11.53am
To: David Thorne
Subject: Re: Re: Re: Re: Re: Re: Timesheets

Good. I wont have to see your ugly head if you go early. Youre the one who will get in trouble dickhead.

....

From: David Thorne
Date: Monday 13 February 2012 12.09pm
To: Simon Dempsey
Subject: Re: Re: Re: Re: Re: Re: Re: Timesheets

Attached image: Foyer2.jpg

Don't shoot yourself accidently in the head moron

The photo above of Kenny from his Facebook profile (which lists his hobbies as hunting, belt carving, and listening to rock'n'roll), was either taken in the 70's or Kenny takes really good care of his glasses.

I have no idea what belt carving is but Kenny is probably a member of a belt carving club where he and fellow belt carving enthusiasts meet regularly to discuss belt carving and their right to carve belts. Kenny is also a member of the National Rifle Association.

I'm not a huge fan of joining clubs. That's not to say my hobbies and interests aren't varied, I just don't want to hang out with people like Kenny.

From: Kenneth Saunders
Date: Sunday 18 November 2012 5.19pm
To: David Thorne
Subject: Your website.

In the US we have a little something called the constitution. Try reading the second amendment. You arent even from this country so you have no idea what you are talking about. Educate yourself or shut the fuck up.

"The right of the people to keep and bear arms shall not be infringed."
James Madison

From: David Thorne
Date: Monday 19 November 2012 11.26am
To: Kenneth Saunders
Subject: Re: Your website.

Dear Kenny,

Thank you for your email. It is always nice to hear from someone with a clear and concise point. I assume you know what it was. Keep up the good fight.

Regards, David.

"If I'm not back in five minutes, just wait longer." Ace Ventura

From: Kenneth Saunders
Date: Monday 19 November 2012 1.04pm
To: David Thorne
Subject: Re: Re: Your website.

I was refering to the story about George and his gun that Carol from work emailed me. A well regulated militia being necessary to the security of a free state, the right of the people to keep and bear arms shall not be infringed. Its the second amendment. Try attending one of the local NRA evenings and educating yourself. Theres enough uneducated gun control lobbyists in the US without you commenting.

....

From: David Thorne
Date: Monday 19 November 2012 1.49pm
To: Kenneth Saunders
Subject: Re: Re: Re: Your website.

Hello Kenny,

At no time in that article did I declare a stance for gun control. I simply mentioned that it is more acceptable for men in West Virginia to hold guns than hands.

While I appreciate the invite, given the choice between an evening of listening to bearded men named Chuck and Randy compare t-shirts featuring eagles while waiting for the tug-circle to begin, or not doing that, I would pick the latter. That's not to say I would enjoy an evening hearing gun control lobbyists carry on about bubbles and elves or whatever it is they carry on about either. I face-palmed while watching footage of Charlton Heston raise his rifle in the air at a NRA meeting declaring, "From my cold dead hands" but my first thought when I read that Rosie O'Donnell was a spokesperson for gun control was 'well, that's enough reason to buy a gun right there.'

Although I have not read the entire constitution, I am familiar with the second amendment as my neighbour has the bumper sticker on his Ford F-350. His name is Terry and he collects tyres. Once, when we took our bins out at the same time, I asked him what all the tyres were for and he replied, "Wouldn't you like to know?"

While it could be argued that a document pertaining to the needs of a young society might not necessarily mirror the needs of that society two-hundred years later, having something to wave around during a debate to save constructing your own rationalisations must be quite handy.

I usually just wave around my arms. Sometimes, if I am particularly annoyed, it can appear as though I am being attacked by bees. It's always important to get your point across in a clear and concise manner.

Regards, David.

From: Kenneth Saunders
Date: Monday 19 November 2012 2.17pm
To: David Thorne
Subject: Re: Re: Re: Re: Your website.

Youve never been to an NRA meeting so keep your mouth shut about things you know nothing about. The NRA protects the right to keep and bear arms which is a part of the constitution. If the government tried to ban cars because some people use them rob banks you'd be the first to cry out for someone to protect your rights. Your either for gun control or against it. Which is it?

From: David Thorne
Date: Monday 19 November 2012 2.51pm
To: Kenneth Saunders
Subject: Re: Re: Re: Re: Re: Your website.

Dear Kenny,

It depends on your definition. I can't think of any reason to own a fully equipped Boeing AH-64 Apache attack helicopter but if I am ever stuck on an island with a group of people who have pointy sticks, I'm going to make a pointy stick.

Decreasing the availability of something rarely decreases a market for it and it is not the availability of firearms that is the issue, it is the availability of idiots. Some form of balance between education and legislation is required. The government doesn't ban cars just because they are sometimes used illegally but they do make you wear seat belts. Blaming a gun for someone being shot may be like blaming a fork for making Rosie O'Donnell fat but limiting her access to the cutlery drawer couldn't hurt. It may be suggested that educating her on the dangers of obesity might be as effective as blocking the availability of forks, but that would require far more effort.

Differentiating between those who purchase forks for collections, sports, or home protection and those who like to eat in front of the mirror would be a difficult task so a nationwide ban would probably be the easiest solution. This may of course create a multi-billion dollar underground market for utensils and years of debate over whether chopsticks fall under fork control legislation but at least we could sleep secure in our beds knowing Rosie isn't shoveling cake into her mouth.

Coming from a country that introduced some of the world's most restrictive firearms legislation to ensure only the police and criminals have them, my first purchase after becoming a US resident was a 1911 stainless Colt Commander. I'm not overly interested in shooting it but I like mechanical things and have spent many hours changing the sights, trigger, mainspring housing, safety, hammer and beaver tail. My second purchase was a Dremel.

It does not automatically mean I wish to accompany you to your weekly hoedown or shop for matching Wrangler jeans together.

Regards, David.

....

From: Kenneth Saunders
Date: Tuesday 20 November 2012 10.14am
To: David Thorne
Subject: Re: Re: Re: Re: Re: Re: Your website.

You own a firearm? What a fucking hypocrite. Once your rights are taken away they arent coming back so you should be supporting the NRA not talking shit on them. Silence is wose than. Its your association representing you in Washington.

....

From: David Thorne
Date: Tuesday 20 November 2012 10.38am
To: Kenneth Saunders
Subject: Re: Re: Re: Re: Re: Re: Re: Your website.

Dear Kenny,

Nobody is arguing that silence isn't wose than. I just have my doubts that those representing gun legislation in Washington are sitting there thinking, 'Where's David? Why isn't he carrying on like a pork chop? He could learn a lot from Kenny.'

While I understand that if someone isn't yelling it can't possibly be important, eventually yelling becomes the normal level and you just turn up the television. For years I thought my grandfather felt strongly about everything but it turned out he was just deaf and gave a fuck about very little.

How about I exercise my right to write, regardless of the possibility of the content being misconstrued by mountain men, and you exercise your right to not click on any more links Carol from work sends you.

Regards, David.

From: Kenneth Saunders
Date: Tuesday 20 November 2012 10.44am
To: David Thorne
Subject: Re: Re: Re: Re: Re: Re: Re: Re: Your website.

Dont shoot yourself accidently in the head moron.

From: David Thorne
Date: Tuesday 20 November 2012 11.18am
To: Kenneth Saunders
Subject: Re: Re: Re: Re: Re: Re: Re: Re: Re: Your website.

Dear Kenny,

You should pitch that to the NRA as their new slogan. I have attached a quick mockup for your presentation.

Regards, David.

From: Kenneth Saunders
Date: Tuesday 20 November 2012 11.50am
To: David Thorne
Subject: Re: Re: Re: Re: Re: Re: Re: Re: Re: Re: Your website.

Blocked.

....

From: David Thorne
Date: Tuesday 20 November 2012 12.24pm
To: Kenneth Saunders
Subject: Re: Re: Re: Re: Re: Re: Re: Re: Re: Re: Re: Your website.

Dear Kenny,

You are aware that simply writing the word 'blocked' doesn't actually do anything aren't you?

Regards, David.

....

From: Kenneth Saunders
Date: Tuesday 20 November 2012 1.09pm
To: David Thorne
Subject: Re: Re: Re: Re: Re: Re: Re: Re: Re: Re: Re: Re: Your website.

Blocked.

Ten reasons I probably shouldn't be alive:
Wilma Deering

During primary school, my second favourite television show was a program called Buck Rogers in the 25th Century which featured a pudgy astronaut named Buck who is frozen is space while testing a new spacecraft and thawed out hundreds of years later when everyone wears really tight jumpsuits. The series followed Buck's many exciting adventures in which he tried to fit into 25th-Century culture, aided by a robot named Twiki and his friend and semi-romantic interest, Colonel Wilma Deering, who wore a tighter jumpsuit than anyone else.

I liked Colonel Wilma Deering a lot. I have seen photos of her since and she isn't much chop but there is no accounting for the logic of prepubescent boys. I had a poster of her on my bedroom wall and I'm fairly sure I kissed it a few times. I also grew fairly resentful of Buck as they spent a lot of time together.

Once, I used a cassette recorder to record myself saying, in a girl's voice, "Buck and I are just friends, I love you David. I want to marry you" and sat there for hours looking at the poster while playing, rewinding, and playing the recording over again. Once, while occupied by my own thoughts during a school class, I called the teacher Wilma which was almost as embarrassing as the times I had previously called her mum.

As the concept of being frozen and later thawed seemed scientifically sound, I decided to undertake the process one night figuring even if Colonel Wilma Deering wasn't going to be waiting for me in the future, there would obviously be a lot of other girls in really tight jumpsuits. Wanting to fit in when I reached the future, I donned my sister's shiny blue spandex unitard and waited patiently until I was sure my parents were asleep before making my way down the hall and into the kitchen.

Opening the refrigerator, I quietly removed the food and the shelves, sat inside, and swung the door shut. Bored and uncomfortable after five minutes, I got out, grabbed a cushion, flashlight and Phantom comic, and climbed back in.

I am not sure if it was due to the lack of air or hypothermia setting in but I remember the shivering stopping and a feeling of warmth settling over me as I began to drift off, happy in the knowledge that the next time I opened my eyes, it would be to the sight of jetpacks, robots and tight jumpsuits.

It was then that I heard the muffled voice of my father, who had risen to use the bathroom and discovered the kitchen floor covered in food, muttering "what the fuck is going on here?" before throwing open the refrigerator door to reveal me sitting on a cushion holding a flashlight and comic book, dressed in my sister's jazzercise outfit.

While one might expect most parents to be angered by this seemingly irrational type of behaviour, years of such had worn my father down to the point where he simply stared at me with a disappointed look on his face before stating, "Stop being a dickhead" and closed the refrigerator door.

While on the subject of Buck Rogers, I once constructed an electric sword after viewing an episode of Buck Rogers where they fought with such. Connecting an old electric car antenna I found in the shed to the house mains and holding it with a garden glove, I tested it on my sister's cat. After dissembling the sword to hide all evidence and opening the windows in an attempt to air out the smell of burnt hair and cooked flesh, I buried (the appropriately named) Sooty in the backyard. A week later, during a family barbecue, the dog dug her up.

Also, while writing this article about Wilma Deering and letting Holly read it, she asked me, "What's a Phantom comic, is it a comic about ghosts?" and I responded, "No, it's a comic about a guy who people think is a ghost because he wears the same costume his ancestors have worn for over four hundred years. He is actually the 21st in a line of crimefighters that originated in 1536, when the father of Christopher Walker was killed during a pirate attack. Swearing an oath to fight evil on the skull of his father's murderer, Christopher started the legacy of the Phantom that would be passed from father to son, leaving people to believe he is immortal. He lives in a cave shaped like a skull." Holly then stared at me with a pitying look so I asked "What?" and she replied, "You are such a geek. Did you dress up like him?" and I lied and said, "No, don't be ridiculous."

The above makes me sound like one of those fat guys with a goatee that collects comic books and argues on forums about who would win in a fight between Batman and Manbat, or whatever, but this is not the case. The only comic books I have ever really read are The Phantom, 2000AD and, more recently, The Walking Dead. I was ten when I discovered The Phantom and living in a small coal mining town that only had one store named, imaginatively, 'The Store' which multitasked as post office, supermarket, video rental (Beta only, twelve to choose from), and newsagent. The only comic they stocked, thrown in between the Trading Post and auto magazines, was The Phantom.

Bored at the store one afternoon, as my mother chatted with Bev, the old lady who served behind the counter, I flicked through the comic and was instantly addicted.

Margin note:

My first favourite show was a series called Blake's 7 because of the spaceship

and a character named Travis who wore an eyepatch and had a gun in his ring. I made an eyepatch and wore it around but my dad told to take it off and stop being a dickhead which is a phrase he favoured. I also liked Avon who would say things like "I'm not stupid; I'm not expendable; and I'm not going."

I have watched the series since and it is as bad as it sounds. I didn't notice the strings on the spaceship when I was young but this was probably due to our television being a 14 inch Rank Arena with a resolution of around 4lpi.

My parents went out to buy a new TV once but came back with a waterbed instead and I remember thinking wtf?

The Phantom lived on a secret island that had gold for sand with a wolf named Devil and a horse named Hero. Even though he could have probably sold some of the gold sand and lived in a mansion, he spent most of his time punching criminals. When he punched them, his special skull ring, that was also some kind of tattooing device, left a permanent skull print on the face of the criminal. Despite how lame it all sounds as I am writing this, at the time I thought it was pretty much the most awesome thing I had ever read. I looked around to make sure nobody in the store was watching, and, shoplifting for the second time in my life, quickly slid the comic under my t-shirt.

The first thing I ever shoplifted was a small metal model of the The Liberator from the science fiction series Blake's 7. Discovering the model while shopping with my mother a year or so before the Phantom comic incident, I asked her to purchase it and she refused, so I stuck it down the back of my pants. On the ride home, the Liberator's front antenna pierced my left buttock but I didn't say anything. When we arrived home, I buried the ship in the soil outside my bedroom window so that it wouldn't be found by my parents and I would know it was close by. It was my most prized possession for about two years. When we moved house, I tried to locate it but it had rusted away.

With the Phantom comic hidden under my t-shirt, I approached my mother at the counter and she turned to me, pointed at my stomach, and said, "What's that?" Looking down, I realised the comic book cover was perfectly visible through the thin white t-shirt I was wearing. "What's The Phantom?" My mother added "and why do you have it under your..." "Oh yes," I quickly interjected, taking the comic out from under my t-shirt, "Can I have this? I was holding it in my shirt because I needed my hands free to scratch my hair. A kid at school today had nits. There is a note from the teacher in my bag." There was an awkward silence as both my mother and the shop assistant stared at me in a similar way to how Holly did when I explained what The Phantom was. Grabbing the comic out of my hands and rolling it into a tube, my mother whacked me across the head with it before placing it on the counter and saying, "and the comic thanks Bev." Not a lot was said on the ride home.

I made myself a Phantom costume that afternoon. The real Phantom's outfit consisted of a purple unitard, with a bit that covered his head, a black mask, stripey black and grey underpants, boots, and a holster with gun.

While not quite the right colour, my sister's shiny blue spandex jazzercise outfit was again put to good use. I would like to say I only ever wore that unitard twice in my life but it was probably more like fifteen times because I thought it was pretty neat. The only pair of striped underpants I owned were orange and green but they did the trick.

To create the bit that went over the Phantom's head, I cut the arm off a blue sweater, tied a knot in one end, pulled it over my head, and cut a hole out where my face was. Two holes cut in one of my sister's cloth headbands served as a mask and my mother's knee high black boots, from the sixties and the back of her wardrobe, were almost identical to the Phantom's boots apart from the three inch heels.

To complete the ensemble, I tied a plastic gun to my waist with packaging string and placed a large metal nut (with a skull drawn on it with a Sharpie) on my finger.

Checking the finished result in the mirror, I convinced myself that if I wasn't me and I saw me walking down the street, probably at night in an alley or something, I would think I was the real Phantom. I imagined stopping a crime and, while being interviewed on the news, taking off my mask and saying "It's me!" to the shock and awe of all the kids at my school.

Removing and hiding the costume under my bed, I decided I would climb out my bedroom window later that night and patrol the streets. Around 8pm, I told my parents, "Well, I'm feeling very sleepy so I'll be going to bed. Don't check on me because I'm going straight to sleep and opening my door might wake me up." After putting on my costume, and placing a pile of clothes under my blanket in case my parents ignored my instructions, I climbed out of my window and ran down the dark street as quickly as I could in three inch heels.

I had never been out alone at night and, being a small town, there were no street lights. Also, while this may not be relative, the night before I had watched a movie called Tarantula about a town that is attacked by giant tarantulas. Admonishing the comic for failing to mention how scary crimefighting at night is, I decided to enlist my friend Ashley in the activity.

Hurrying to his house, I jumped over his side fence (dropping into a crouching stance and whispering "The Phantom!"), climbed up onto the water tank below his bedroom window, and tapped several times.

Ashley pulled his curtains apart and looked out to see someone in a mask, with a sock pulled over their head tied at the top, staring back at him with a finger to their lips saying "Shhhh." His whole face went bigger and he screamed. At the same time, he did some kind of spasmodic dance and then disappeared from the window. Panicking, I jumped down from the water tank and ran. I could hear his screams continuing from within the house as I jumped the side fence and bolted down the street towards home.

The next day, Ashley wasn't at school. Around lunch time, our class was visited by Sergeant Robertson (the town police officer and fire chief), who gave a talk on Stranger Danger and explained why our classmate was away that day. He then showed us a picture Ashley had drawn of the person he saw outside his window. It was pretty bad. I'm not saying I am the best drawer in the world but even by eight year old standards it was pretty bad.

It looked like a corn cob wearing black rimmed glasses. The Sergeant asked us if we had ever seen anyone dressed similarly and, unimpressed by the drawing, I put my hand up and answered, "If Ashley wasn't such a bad drawer, it would probably look a bit like the Phantom."

Sergeant Robinson: Who's the phantom?

Me: "A crimefighter. He lives in a skull."

Sergeant Robinson: "In a what?"

Me : "A skull."

Sergeant Robinson: "What are you talking about?"

Me : "It's a big cave shaped like a skull. He lives in it."

Sergeant Robinson: "No, I mean are you talking about a cartoon or something?"

Me : "No, it's a comic."

Sergeant Robinson: "And he wears a mask?"

Me : "Yes."

Sergeant Robinson: "Have you ever dressed up like him and visited a friends house at night?"

Me : "... No."

The moment the end of school bell rang, I ran home, returned my sister's unitard to the dirty laundry basket, and hid the remaining evidence at the back of our shed behind a mini-bike and Slip'n'Slide.

Ashley returned to school a few days later. His mother walked him to and from school after that and he spent recess and lunch in the library for the rest of the year, but he seemed to prefer it that way so it all worked out fine in the end. I sent him a Facebook friend request recently with the message, "Hey remember me? And I don't mean from the night you looked out your window and saw the Phantom" but he blocked me.

Connect the dots
to discover a fucking triangle

Bill tries
to buy cheese
#3

I know you are busy, so I made another form for you to fill out

I don't like Microsoft Word. As a designer and Mac user, the only time I ever have to open Word is when some idiot sends me an attachment in Word format. Melissa once emailed me a copy of an email as a word document. The word document contained a jpg screenshot of the original email. I am deleting Word from my computer after I finish writing this line.

From: Melissa Peters
Date: Monday 27 February 2012 9.38am
To: All staff
Subject: Form

Hi,

I know everyone is really busy this week trying to get the annual report layout done on time so I will get everyone their lunches this week and bring them back instead of everyone having to go to the shops themselves. There is a lunch order form attached in Word format. Just print it out and write down what you want and leave it on my desk. I'll write in the price when I am at the shops and at the end of the week i'll work out your total.

Thanks Mel

....

From: David Thorne
Date: Monday 27 February 2012 9.47am
To: Melissa Peters
Subject: Re: Form

Dear Melissa,

While I appreciate your efforts to improve productivity by removing the only half hour reprieve I get each day, couldn't I just tell you what I want and you write it down?

Regards, David.

From: Melissa Peters
Date: Monday 27 February 2012 9.54am
To: David Thorne
Subject: Re: Re: Form

No because then I would have to write everyones down. It is quicker if you all do it yourselves.

Mel

....

From: David Thorne
Date: Monday 27 February 2012 9.57am
To: Melissa Peters
Subject: Re: Re: Re: Form

How long did it take you to make the form in Word?

....

From: Melissa Peters
Date: Monday 27 February 2012 10.02am
To: David Thorne
Subject: Re: Re: Re: Re: Form

Can you just fill it out please?

....

From: David Thorne
Date: Monday 27 February 2012 10.42am
To: Melissa Peters
Subject: Re: Re: Re: Re: Re: Form

Of course. Please find attached. I thought it would be quicker to scan and attach as a password protected .RAR file than put it on your desk. The password is Fritter. I apologise for the delay in getting it back to you, I had to load Word, work out how to print from Word, install printer drivers for Word, reboot Word and load the typeface you used in Word, before I could print and fill it out.

I will mark the forty minutes down on my time sheets as Melissalaneous.

Regards, David.

Margin note:

Melissa's favourite movie is "the Twilight series" which explains a lot. I was actually at the cinema while Twilight was showing - to watch a different movie not featuring sparkly vampires - and ordered a large coke. Not realising I was expected to select between two Twilight branded plastic cups, when asked "Team Edward or Team Jacob?" I replied "Team couldn't care less" and was given a Sex in the City cup which was probably meant to teach me a lesson but, given a choice between a movie about four middle aged women discussing vaginas and shoes or one about self obsessed whiney teens riding piggy-back through forests, I would just pick the shortest.

LUNCH ORDER FORM

ORDER	
NAME	David Thorne

DATE	27 / 02 / 2012

ORDER	PRICE:
Milk	
Bread	
Confetti	
Mayonaise (Kraft original)	
Pickles	
Window cleaner	
Butter	
Tomatoes	
Oven Mittens	
Basil	
Mozarella cheese	
Beer	
Keurig K-cups (Black Tiger by Coffee People)	
Chips	
A t-shirt with a dragon on it	
Sour cream	
TOTAL	

From: Melissa Peters
Date: Monday 27 February 2012 10.51am
To: David Thorne
Subject: Re: Re: Re: Re: Re: Re: Form

I'm not doing your supermarket shopping for you and you're meant to print it out not email it to me. If you email it to me I will just have to print it out. The form is for lunch from the deli down the road. Just things from there. They have sandwiches and stuff.

Mel

. . . .

From: David Thorne
Date: Monday 27 February 2012 10.56am
To: Melissa Peters
Subject: Re: Re: Re: Re: Re: Re: Re: Form

Those sandwiches sound alright. I'll just have one of them.

. . . .

From: Melissa Peters
Date: Monday 27 February 2012 11.02am
To: David Thorne
Subject: Re: Re: Re: Re: Re: Re: Re: Re: Form

Then write what you want on the form! That's the whole point of it. Why is it so confusing for you? Everyone else has filled out theirs.

Mel

. . . .

From: David Thorne
Date: Monday 27 February 2012 11.33am
To: Melissa Peters
Subject: Attached revised order in .EPS format

LUNCH ORDER FORM

NAME	David Thorne

DATE	27 / 02/ 2012

ORDER	Just a sandwich thanks.	PRICE:
	TOTAL	

From: Melissa Peters
Date: Monday 27 February 2012 11.41am
To: David Thorne
Subject: Re: Attached revised order in .EPS format

What kind of sandwich? What do you want in it? I'm not a mind reader. You have to write down exactly what you want. Everyone else has written down exactly what they want on theirs. I'm doing this to help you know. Ive got better things to do with my time than get you lunch. If you don't want to fill out the form then you will have to go out and get your own lunch. I'm going out at 12.30

From: David Thorne
Date: Monday 27 February 2012 11.46am
To: Melissa Peters
Subject: Re: Re: Attached revised order in .EPS format

Nice day for it. I'd probably pop out myself for a break if I wasn't so busy with all these forms to complete. If you are going anywhere near a hardware store, would you be able to get me a key cut? For anywhere, I don't mind.

From: Melissa Peters
Date: Monday 27 February 2012 11.55am
To: David Thorne
Subject: Re: Re: Re: Attached revised order in .EPS format

Im not going anywhere near a hardware store. I'm going to get lunch for everyone at 12.30 from the shops down the road. I'm not driving anywhere. Do you want something for lunch or not? You've got about 30 minutes to fill in the form or you can get your own lunch. If you just write I want a sandwich or whatever dumb shit you want without being exact then I'm not getting you anything.

From: David Thorne
Date: Monday 27 February 2012 12.27pm
To: Melissa Peters
Subject: Attached revised order v.2 in layered .PSD format

LUNCH ORDER FORM

NAME David Thorne

DATE 27 / 02 / 2012

ORDER 1 x Sandwich.   **PRICE:**

The sandwich should
consist of two slices of
fresh white bread (a) and
(b), with the following
produce inbetween:

(c) 1 x slice of swiss cheese
(d) 8 x shakes of pepper
(e) 1 x thin slice of tomato
(f) 1 x small amount of
butter per inward facing
surface of each slice
of bread.

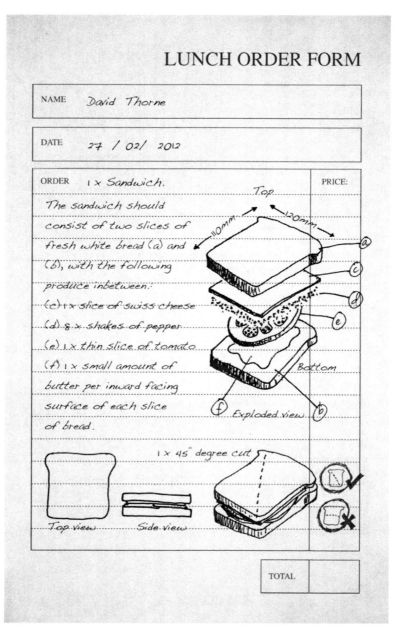

Top

110mm   120mm

(a)
(c)
(d)
(e)

Bottom

(f)   Exploded view   (b)

1 x 45° degree cut

Top view   Side view

TOTAL

Wyndham&Miller™

ATT: David Thorne
RE: Invoices
DATE: Sep 14 2012

Dear David,

Last Thursday you were given the task of organizing Kevin's office birthday party due to Melissa being on annual leave. The budget you were given of $1000 was meant to be for catering. We assumed you would also organize CDs for the music.

I have checked with the accounts department and you managed to go over budget by $1155.25 which includes:

$375.00 I day hire of inflatable jumping castle from Amusements Unlimited

$125.00 1 hour appearance of clown from Big Country Amusements

$125.00 1 hour appearance by face painter from Big Country Amusements

$85.00 1/2 hour appearance by mime from Big Country Amusements

$55.00 charge for helium and balloon animals from Big Country Amusements

$240.00 1 hour hire of Shetland pony from Big Country Amusements

$273.85 for pizzas from Dominos

$412.70 for cartons of beer from Murphy's Hotel

$230.20 for cartons of cigarettes from Murphy's Hotel

$33.50 Assorted party hats from Target

$200.00 2 hour hire of your niece Lauren to play music on her flute

$2155.25 Total

In future, if you are ever given the task of organizing events again, you are to check with the accounts department BEFORE you order and pay for any deliveries or services.

Sincerely

Jennifer Haines
Human Resources Manager
Wyndham Miller

Wyndham Miller & Associates 3rd Floor, 926B Massachusetts Avenue NW, Washington DC 20036
Tel +1 202 630 9372 **Fax** +1 202 630 9380 **Web** wyndhammiller.com

140

Ten reasons I probably shouldn't be alive:
The beach

I don't like the beach. I especially dislike busy beaches and having to navigate through eight thousand people to find a metre squared plot in which to take my top off in front of eight thousand people before venturing into a body of water with eight thousand people. Brochures always show beaches deserted, possibly with a footprint in the sand, but they are never like that. I would probably quite like the beach if there wasn't any people. Or sharks. A private beach would be quite nice, one a few steps down from a mansion of something. I probably wouldn't actually go swimming but I might sit on the bottom step eating a sandwich while looking out at the water. Probably wondering how many sharks are just below the surface and what type. Then I would go back up to my mansion and read a newspaper or something while wearing one of those white bath-robes.

Once, while at the beach with my offspring, I swam out past eight thousand people and waved. Interpreting my waving for drowning, two huge men, wearing red shorts and carrying surfboards, bolted down the beach, dove in and swam towards me. To escape, I dove as they approached but one reached under the surface and grabbed my foot - causing me to hang upside down and swallow water. Gasping to the surface, I was met by the other man pushing a surfboard towards me, which hit me in the side of the head.

While the next few moments were a semi-concious blur of waves crashing and losing my shorts while being pulled over a surfboard, I recovered lying on the beach in the centre of an applauding crowd with my genitals covered by an old lady's sun hat. Wrapping a borrowed Spongebob Squarepants towel around my lower half, I waded back into the water in search of my shorts and was stung by a jellyfish.

I went to the beach again recently, after managing to avoid the whole process for several years, and regardless of the fact that there is no logical purpose for a bee to be at the beach, I was stung by one on the face.

Simon giving oral sex to a rabbit.

141

Forged almost entirely from thermoplastic polymers, David Thorne Hums the Theme From Space 1999 and Other Christmas Classics contains over 26 popular Christmas tracks such as the theme from that movie about the big boat and that other one about the two guys.

REVIEWS

Thanks for the xmas present dichead. Is this really the kind of thing you do in your spare time? You need to get a life. I listened to about 1 second of it and threw it in the bin. Don't send me your stupid shit and I expect the stuff about me on the website to be deleted. I spoke to a lawyer and he said I could sue you for defamation.

Lucius Thaller, Courier

What the fuck is this supposed to be? I played it in the car on the way to work and it is just you humming. I put up with it for about 10 seconds and skipped to the next track and it is just more humming. The whole thing is you humming.

Simon Dempsey, Horse whisperer

Not interested in your rubbish. Next time you think "I will send Peter something stupid" just dont.

Peter Williams, Real Estate Agent

I got your present today. Is this really a whole CD of you humming? None of the songs on it are even Christmas songs apart from track 4 the one about the tree and I can hear you making a coffee and stirring it. Is this really my xmas present?

Melissa Peters, Receptionist

How is the Neighbours theme a christmas song? And you called it "A song about people by that guy". Worst cd I have ever heard.

Jason Lowe, Magazine Editor

Thanks for the CD. Just thought you might like to know that you can hear a dog barking outside on the track called That exciting bit in Excalibur.

Jennifer Haines, Human Resources Officer

Davey. This disk of you humming is a joke? Nobody will buy a cd of someone humming. You are not even humming christmas songs. You should buy a guitar and I will teach you how to play.

Jon de Peinder, Designer

Man that is just sad. I lol'd and then I put it on and listened to it and I was embarrassed for you. Did you seriously sit there and hum the whole thing? I was pushing the next button every time you started humming. I don't even want it in the house in case someone accidentally plays it again.

Mark Pearcy, Designer

Hi, I got your cd in the post today. If this is really my present I hope you are not expecting anything good from me this year.

1. It is just humming.
2. The cover photo and track titles are just tragic.
3. It says Christmas but there are no christmas songs.
4. The back titles just say "that song from that thing" etc.
5. You can hear you washing dishes and stuff.

Jenny Leavesly, Photographer

Wow. More proof that you really are a complete moron. A whole cd of you humming? I hope you sank a lot of money into this and starve to death.

Robert Schaefer, Managing Director

Received your christmas present. You should definately get some kind of professional help. How much did this cost you to make?

Mike Campbell, Art Director

Merry Christmas to you too and thanks for the music cd. One of the guys came in to see what I listening to and he said it sounded like you were one of those kids with down syndrome.

Jaimie Holding, Copy writer

Thanks for the worst cd ever created in the history of cds. I would rather listen to monkeys screaming.

Brian Mitchell, Accountant

How long did it take you to do this? This is exactly the kind of thing I was talking about. If you took as much time filling in your time sheets as fucking about you would get along fine. Did you do this during work hours? Is that you humming on the disk? You sound like an idiot.

Kevin Eastwood, Account Rep

World's worst Christmas album. Ever.

Andrew Whittaker, Programmer

Could only listen to about 10 seconds of each song before I began to twitch.

Gina Caretti, Production Manager

Hi. I got your package this morning. Pretty terrible. On track 4 you can hear you doing things in the sink. It sounds like you are washing dishes or something. On track 2 you can hear a dog barking in the background and there is lots of stuff in the other tracks. I can hear you lighting a cigarette in one of them. If you set out to make the lamest CD ever you have done a pretty good job.

Jodie Williams, Graphic Designer

Employee Self Evaluation Form

E34-F

Instructions for completing this form

Please complete this self evaluation form prior to your formal performance review and return
to the Human Resources Department. Your answers will be discussed in your review session.
Please retain a copy for your records. If you have any questions regarding the completion
of this form, please see your supervisor or the Human Resources department.

Date Oct/ 8 / 2012	**Employee Name** David Thorne
Job Title Copy writer / design director / office slut	
Department Design	**Supervisor** Geordi La Forge

Rating

Excellent Performs all tasks in an exceptional manner.
Good Performs many tasks well, all other tasks adequately and requires little supervision.
Satisfactory Performs all tasks satisfactorily and requires occasional supervision.
Unsatisfactory Fails to perform many tasks and requires regular supervision.

---

1. Procedures met Review procedures you have met during the last 12 months.

Comments My daily 10.30 procedure of watching Jodie consume cake
while complaining about not being able to lose weight was met 70
percent of the time. I was absent the other 30% but I assume Jodie
still ate cake. Her procedure of wearing stretchy bike-pants despite
obviously having never been near a bike was also met.

☒ all of the above
☐ Excellent
☐ Good
☐ Satisfactory
☐ Unsatisfactory

---

2. Procedures implemented Review procedures you have implemented during the last 12 months

Comments I attempted to implement a daily procedure of
co-worker bonding whereby we stop work half an hour before
closing and spend 15 minutes insulting each other and then another
15 minutes apologising for the terrible things that were said. Staff
enthusiasm and adoption of this procedure was disappointing.

☒ gift certicate
☐ Excellent
☐ Good
☐ Satisfactory
☐ Unsatisfactory

3. Objectives met Review objectives you have met during the last 12 months.

Comments My objective of having my monitor positioned where nobody else in the office could see it was met by rotating my desk two inches per day over a three month period so that nobody would notice. I also placed a plant on my desk to point at in case anyone asked, "is something different in here?"

- [x] select track
- [ ] Excellent
- [ ] Good
- [ ] Satisfactory
- [ ] Unsatisfactory

4. Future objectives Review future goals and objectives and your ability to execute these objectives.

Comments If you were to travel back in time to 1012 and show a 2012 John Deere combine harvester to a peasant working the King's land, he would think it was magic. It is therefore difficult to predict what the future will bring. Probably something to do with hover-belts or chickens that cook themselves when you press a button on their head.

- [x] robot servants
- [ ] Excellent
- [ ] Good
- [ ] Satisfactory
- [ ] Unsatisfactory

5. Time management Review your ability/strengths to meet project timelines over the last 12 months.

Comments My ability to construct viable excuses as to why client's projects have not been completed on time is one of my strengths. Usually, I am able to convince the client that it is their fault. If not, I tell them Simon is the one working on their project and we don't like to rush him or he slaps his head and screams.

- [x] included
- [ ] Excellent
- [ ] Good
- [ ] Satisfactory
- [ ] Unsatisfactory

6. Special skills/abilities Review any special skills and/or abilities you may have and how they are utilized.

Comments Telekinesis. The largest object I have been able to move by staring at and concentrating is a Bic pen but I practice at my desk for at least four hours per day on other objects. This would be useful if someone asked to borrow a pen and I was completely paralysed from a trampoline accident or spider bite.

- [x] yes
- [ ] Excellent
- [ ] Good
- [ ] Satisfactory
- [ ] Unsatisfactory

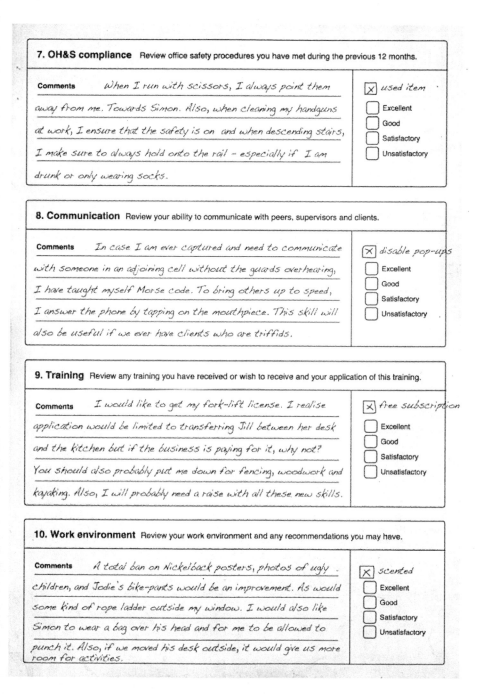

7. OH&S compliance Review office safety procedures you have met during the previous 12 months.

Comments When I run with scissors, I always point them away from me. Towards Simon. Also, when cleaning my handguns at work, I ensure that the safety is on and when descending stairs, I make sure to always hold onto the rail – especially if I am drunk or only wearing socks.

- [x] used item
- [ ] Excellent
- [ ] Good
- [ ] Satisfactory
- [ ] Unsatisfactory

8. Communication Review your ability to communicate with peers, supervisors and clients.

Comments In case I am ever captured and need to communicate with someone in an adjoining cell without the guards overhearing, I have taught myself Morse code. To bring others up to speed, I answer the phone by tapping on the mouthpiece. This skill will also be useful if we ever have clients who are triffids.

- [x] disable pop-ups
- [ ] Excellent
- [ ] Good
- [ ] Satisfactory
- [ ] Unsatisfactory

9. Training Review any training you have received or wish to receive and your application of this training.

Comments I would like to get my fork-lift license. I realise application would be limited to transferring Jill between her desk and the kitchen but if the business is paying for it, why not? You should also probably put me down for fencing, woodwork and kayaking. Also, I will probably need a raise with all these new skills.

- [x] free subscription
- [ ] Excellent
- [ ] Good
- [ ] Satisfactory
- [ ] Unsatisfactory

10. Work environment Review your work environment and any recommendations you may have.

Comments A total ban on Nickelback posters, photos of ugly children, and Jodie's bike-pants would be an improvement. As would some kind of rope ladder outside my window. I would also like Simon to wear a bag over his head and for me to be allowed to punch it. Also, if we moved his desk outside, it would give us more room for activities.

- [x] scented
- [ ] Excellent
- [ ] Good
- [ ] Satisfactory
- [ ] Unsatisfactory

11. Attendance Review your attendance record over the previous 12 months.

Comments I have attended the office 100% of the time that I was not able to come up with a believable excuse for doing something else instead. If I lock my office door and shimmy out the window ten minutes after arriving, it still counts as attending and I actually get a lot more done this way, last week, I painted my outdoor furniture.

- [x] family pack
- [ ] Excellent
- [ ] Good
- [ ] Satisfactory
- [ ] Unsatisfactory

12. Action plan Review any action plans you may have. These will be discussed during your review session.

Comments The main character, a ten year old girl driven by revenge for the killing of her parents, trains as an assassin. There would be a lot of slow motion and maybe a suit that enhances her speed and skills that she builds because she is a genius and can read and memorise a whole book just by flicking through the pages.

- [x] 2 thumbs up
- [ ] Excellent
- [ ] Good
- [ ] Satisfactory
- [ ] Unsatisfactory

13. Additional review Add any additional reviews you may wish to discuss during your review session.

Comments Quite disappointed with this product, hence only giving it two stars; the handle broke off after using it once. I would recommend spending a little more on a quality product. Also, the colour is nothing like the product shown in the photo, the photo shows it as a deep blue and the product is more like a turquoise.

- [ ] Excellent
- [ ] Good
- [ ] Satisfactory
- [ ] Unsatisfactory
- [x] sent back

After completing this form

Please sign and date the completed self-evaluation form and return
to the Human Resources Department.

Signed _David Thorne_   **Date** _Oct 8 / 2012_

More statements my offspring has made

Margin note:

My son Seb has just turned ten and as I am currently at war with the next-door neighbour, his birthday present this year was Guitar Hero. People often complain about how hard it is to raise kids but apart from the occasional school run and, on the odd occasion when he seriously hurts himself, driving him to the bus stop so he can make his way to the hospital, there really isn't that much to it.

"We should get the words 'Bad Boys' on our number plate. That way when people are behind us at the traffic lights, they wont mess with us. If they do, we can just lock the doors."

"We should sell everything we own and use the money to buy something nice instead."

"I can't have a bath. Nobody can. I saw a spider in it yesterday so it will have to be disinfected."

"That actually seems like a good deal to me. I would much rather have magic beans than a cow. Who wouldn't?"

"I will need a black leather jacket. It is part of the new school uniform. I don't even want a black leather jacket but I have to do what the school says."

"I know that Emma likes me because Andrew asked Kate to ask her if she liked me and she said 'no'. If she didn't care she would have said 'he's ok'. Girls do that."

"I don't like Emma anymore, she doesn't get the rules of hand-ball. It's not that hard and I made her a complete list. Tornado's are 10 points, Spinners are 5 and a Benny means everyone moves right one square and is not allowed to speak until the next point.

"What's a brothel? Is it a kind of soup?"

"I've never even heard of Corduroy. I hope you kept the receipt because these pants are going back."

"My teacher has Aunt Jemima." (Turned out it was emphysemia)

"When I am an adult I will go for walks without telling anyone where I am. I will walk into shops and if anyone asks what I doing, I will say "just looking" and then walk back out."

"Is the guy in the wheelchair in Glee acting or is he a real parallelogram?"

Buying a
Canada Goose™ jacket
online

Call me a cynic, but I have my doubts that John was actually emailing me from Canada.

From: David Thorne
Date: Tuesday 8 February 2011 1.10pm
To: John Michaels
Subject: Canada Goose jacket

Hello John,

Can you let me know if the jackets are actual Canada Goose products or Chinese reproductions?

Regards, David.

....

From: John Michaels
Date: Tuesday 8 February 2011 3.13pm
To: David Thorne
Subject: Re: Canada Goose jacket

No made in china. Made in Canada. In 1957, the city was founded in Toronto, Canada flourish in the textile industry. The brand launched by the company CANADA GOOSE is. It is high brand of many claps.

You outdoor brands move production to other countries in Asia and the earth in order to promote value for money and be still to look beautiful, I stick to innovate technology and product is always strong. I promise. Standing higher than 50 years since its founding, CANADA GOOSE Product of Siberia and northern Canada, and the people living in a cold land, such as Alaska, Antarctic expedition, Snowy lands with wind and ice and animals. No to the wind. I will not be cold. Feedback has been based on data from the product of real experience in their field it is. I promise.

High-quality functionality and comfort with solid technical force, has received high praise from humans of the world it is. There are no lies.

Buying an Omega Speedmaster Pro™ online

I don't actually know why or how it happened. One moment I was looking at an expensive watch on Amazon, and the next I had clicked the 'Buy with 1 click' button. Instantly experiencing the sweaty, panicky version of buyer's remorse, I considered calling the bank and reporting the credit card stolen but it is unlikely they would believe a robber, in possession of my card, would log in to my Amazon account and order me a watch. My second thought was to call Amazon and cancel the order but this would mean I wouldn't actually get the watch.

Boys like watches. Girls like watches too, but not in the same way as they get to wear as much other jewellery as they want. It takes my partner Holly almost twenty minutes to remove her bracelets going through airport security and if she stood on the roof of our house with her arms outstretched, she would be able to pick up Japanese television broadcasts. Or be struck by lightning. If it was the latter, I wouldn't have to explain the watch.

I probably spend more on Amazon than I do on coffee and cigarettes. Which is saying a lot. In the last month alone, Holly has questioned our bank statement no less than ten times. Having a quick look at last month's Amazon order list, it includes: 4 x pair of Explorer socks, 1 x Babolat tennis racquet, 3 x John Wyndham novels, 1 x Banksy book (with a picture of a guy throwing flowers on the cover), 1 x pair of cargo shorts, 1 x Mexican wrestling mask, 1 x tube of Polywatch (a hesalite watch-face scratch remover) and 1 x cast iron toilet roll holder shaped like a giraffe.

I may have some kind of problem.

Also, when I gave a draft of this book to a friend to read, he told me to take out this article because it reads as if I am saying "hey everybody, I have an expensive watch. I am so great!" but I left it in anyway. Because it is the only email between myself and Holly that she has agreed to let me publish.

Her emails usually end with, "and if I find out you posted this anywhere, I will stab you while you're sleeping."

From: Holly Thorne
Date: Thursday 9 June 2011 10.16am
To: David Thorne
Subject: Amazon order

Did you order something from Amazon with the credit card for $2,280 on Tuesday?

Holly

From: David Thorne
Date: Thursday 9 June 2011 10.22am
To: Holly Thorne
Subject: Re: Amazon order

I'm offended by the question. How irresponsible do you think I am?

From: Holly Thorne
Date: Thursday 9 June 2011 10.31am
To: David Thorne
Subject: Re: Re: Amazon order

I'm at work, I don't have time to write the ten pages that question demands. It was charged to the credit card on June 7. If you didn't order something, I will call the bank and find out what's going on. Did you buy something for $2,280 or not?

From: David Thorne
Date: Thursday 9 June 2011 10.42am
To: Holly Thorne
Subject: Re: Re: Re: Amazon order

Yes. But I blame Amazon's 'Buy with 1 click' button. Evaluating the consequences of clicking it takes longer than clicking it and you know how little patience I possess.

You experienced first hand the button's seductive propensity last week when you were browsing for books about glassblowing and purchased a kayak.

Yes, I can hear you Houston. We had a space emergency but everything is ok now. David fixed the airlock seal with his tachymeter.

From: Holly Thorne
Date: Thursday 9 June 2011 10.47am
To: David Thorne
Subject: Re: Re: Re: Re: Amazon order

The kayak was under 300 dollars and you bought a model of the space shuttle and an orange NASA jumpsuit at the same time. At least we can both use the Kayak. It's good to try new things. What the hell did you buy that cost $2280?

Build your own origami International Space Station:

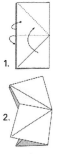

1.

2.

3.

4.

From: David Thorne
Date: Thursday 9 June 2011 10.59am
To: Holly Thorne
Subject: Re: Re: Re: Re: Re: Amazon order

It's not a jumpsuit, it's a flight suit. Discovery doesn't jump into orbit. I purchased an Omega Speedmaster Professional. Apparently it keeps terrible time, can't get wet, has to be wound daily and its Hesalite crystal face scratches in a mild breeze, but it was the first watch worn on the moon.

Buzz Aldrin wore the exact model during the Apollo 11 mission and it has the words 'Flight qualified by NASA for all manned space missions' stamped into the back. It also has a tachymeter.

From: Holly Thorne
Date: Thursday 9 June 2011 11.14am
To: David Thorne
Subject: Re: Re: Re: Re: Re: Re: Amazon order

That will come in handy the next time someone asks "Has anybody got a tachymeter?" I don't care if it was the first watch worn on the sun, $2,280 is a ridiculous amount of money to pay for a watch even if it has a tachymeter.

We're supposed to be saving money, not buying everything that has the NASA logo stuck on it. I'm going to get home one day and find a space shuttle in the driveway and you sitting inside wearing your jumpsuit. When I didn't finish my food at Jalisco's last night you said "There are children in Africa who would kill for that taco." How does a $2,280 watch fit in with your newfound altruism?

From: David Thorne
Date: Thursday 9 June 2011 11.33am
To: Holly Thorne
Subject: Re: Re: Re: Re: Re: Re: Re: Amazon order

I'm pretty sure the kids in Africa would want me to have the watch. And, given the choice between a watch and a taco, I doubt any African child would choose the watch. It's not as if they have business meetings to attend or need to know when it is dinner time.

They could probably use a kayak though. When asked "what's the time?" by passersby, they would reply, from beneath the shade of their new kayak, "Why? Are you late for a business meeting?" and the passersby would respond, "Sarcasm is the lowest form of... is that a taco?"

I'm also fairly sure that if I showed the African kids the watch and asked, "Should I have sent you a cheque instead?" they would reply, "No, charity is detrimental unless it helps the recipient become independent of it. Besides, I'd rather have a taco." They would probably then ask what the tachymeter is for and I would have to admit that I have no idea.

While I am all for altruism, it shouldn't entail exclusive concern for the welfare of others over one's own needs. It is all about balance; I ate all of my tacos so I get a watch. Which, incidently, was actually only $2,100. As it retails for nearly $4000, this means I have effectively saved us nineteen-hundred dollars. If I were to do this every week, by the end of the year we would have saved 4.7 million dollars. We could purchase as much altruism as we want with that kind of cash. And jetpacks. It's good to try new things.

....

From: Holly Thorne
Date: Thursday 9 June 2011 11.41am
To: David Thorne
Subject: Re: Re: Re: Re: Re: Re: Re: Re: Amazon order

4.7 million? Even with a space watch I wouldn't hold your breath waiting for NASA to call as they probably prefer their astronauts to be capable of basic math.

If you were in space and ground control asked you to plot the trajectory for re-entry, everbody would burn. If the watch was only $2,100, what did you buy with the other $180? And does it also have a NASA logo on it?

From: David Thorne
Date: Thursday 9 June 2011 11.44am
To: Holly Thorne
Subject: Re: Re: Re: Re: Re: Re: Re: Re: Re: Amazon order

No, the extra $180 was for a pair of pants.

....

From: Holly Thorne
Date: Thursday 9 June 2011 11.47am
To: David Thorne
Subject: Re: Re: Re: Re: Re: Re: Re: Re: Re: Re: Amazon order

Did Buzz Aldrin wear them on the moon?

Right Wing: **Uri Geller**

Left Wing: **David Copperfield**

Simon giving oral sex to a plane.

David and his best friends go camping

A bit of
an emergency

From: Christopher Gould
Date: Monday 8 Aug 2011 3.06pm
To: David Thorne
Subject: Hi

Got a bit of an emergency. Im getting paid to play games online which is pretty sweet but I need to update my computer. Only need $800 becasue I already have some saved. Would you be able to borrow me it if I paid you back?

From: David Thorne
Date: Tuesday 9 Aug 2011 10.17am
To: Christopher Gould
Subject: Re: Hi

From: Christopher Gould
Date: Tuesday 9 Aug 2011 10.52am
To: David Thorne
Subject: Re: Re: Hi

Fuck you then.

Dressing like a woman doesn't make you special

There are many things to be said for working in the design industry but as they are mostly negative, especially those regarding clients, I would rather write about robots.

If I was a robot, programmed to serve people all day, I would throw myself off a cliff. Working in the design industry is a lot like being a robot. A robot that curses its positronic brain for not allowing it to ignore the first law and attach spinning blades to its arms and take out the next human that states "that's nice but can we try it in green?" or "can you make the text bigger?" Actually, scratch that, working in the design industry is more like being a whore. A dirty whore who has programmed its mind to find a happy place rather than be outraged by client requests. There are many things to be said for working in the design industry but mostly that it is like being a dirty robot whore.

I was once yelled at by a client for not being able to create an animated video of two cars talking to eachother for their website "like Disney does" by that afternoon. Another time, during a presentation, the client actually started crying because they were "expecting something good." Just last week, a client asked me to send them a file in 'Ready, Set, Go' format.

From: Robert Schaefer
Date: Monday 8 November 2010 9.11am
To: David Thorne
Subject: Artwork

Hello David,

Can you send me the artwork for our business cards you did last year. Finsbury Press has asked for the original files. I need the artwork by Wednesday so either this afternoon or tomorrow is fine.

Thanks Rob

From: David Thorne
Date: Monday 8 November 2010 10.24am
To: Robert Schaefer
Subject: Re: Artwork

Hello Bob,

I have received your email but no longer work for that agency. Due to client account management resembling that German dance where men in tights slap each other, the company was basically trading insolvent and I resigned.

While some may see this as the proverbial rat deserting a sinking ship, I prefer to think of it as quietly stepping out of a bathtub you have been sharing with four retarded children while they are busy arguing over who lost the soap. I would suggest contacting the agency and requesting your business card artwork before the owner swaps the art department computers for magic beans.

Alternatively, if you would like me to recreate and send the files to you, I would be happy to help. I estimate this would take three hours at seventy five dollars per hour.

Regards, David.

From: Robert Schaefer
Date: Monday 8 November 2010 12.17pm
To: David Thorne
Subject: Re: Re: Artwork

It's Rob not Bob and I already emailed them and they said they don't have the files and to contact you. I'm not paying you $225 for artwork when I already paid you for the artwork last year.

From: David Thorne
Date: Monday 8 November 2010 3.02pm
To: Robert Schaefer
Subject: Re: Re: Re: Artwork

Dear Bob,

You paid the agency to provide artwork and I no longer work for that agency. While generally a frontline supporter of questioning logic, this support wavers drastically in the face of providing free work.

A few years back, I bought my first four-wheel drive vehicle from a dealership. The salesman who did the paperwork was named Roger. While on a camping trip several months later with my nine year old offspring, I parked the vehicle on a dirt incline near a river and set up the tent. The next morning, we awoke to find it had rained - turning the dirt incline into a slippery mud incline - and the vehicle missing with four tyre-wide grooves leading to the edge of the river. Realising my mobile phone had been on the rear seat of the vehicle along with our box of food, we survived by riding a Coleman® inflatable air mattress down the river for two days to the nearest town. I will admit that during the voyage the thought of eating my offspring crossed my mind on more than one occasion but this was less due to hunger than his constant complaining of "Why do I have to hold on to the back while you ride," "Are we there yet?" and "I can't feel my legs."

Making it home and reporting the vehicle as 'stolen', I went shopping for a new one the following week. I did not to turn up at Roger's front door requesting a replacement vehicle for the one I lost. While it is entirely possible Roger may have nodded, sympathised and explained patiently the structure of modern commerce, it is more likely he would have just called me a dickhead.

Also, while three hours at $75.00 does equate to $225.00, the total cost to recreate and sent your business card artwork would be $450.00 due to the Jumping Frog fee.

Regards, David.

....

From: Robert Schaefer
Date: Monday 8 November 2010 3.18pm
To: David Thorne
Subject: Re: Re: Re: Re: Artwork

You are seriously pissing me off now. I remember you from the meeting you were that idiot wearing a green Atari t-shirt. Im NOT paying for work I have already paid for and 3 hours at $75.00 per hour is $225.00 NOT $450.00 - that is double. where the did you get double from and what the fuck is a jumping frog fee?

Simon giving oral sex to a horse.

From: David Thorne
Date: Monday 8 November 2010 4.46pm
To: Robert Schaefer
Subject: Re: Re: Re: Re: Re: Artwork

Dear Bob,

I remember you from the meeting too (specifically your haggling over pricing and questioning why animated gifs can't be used on your business card) but no, sadly the Atari clad individual would have been Thomas the owner. Nearing forty, he felt retro t-shirts and trucker caps, like the cool kids wear, disguised the fact. Once one has seen his size 40 lower-half squeezed into size 32 skinny jeans like two parallel overflowing cake icing funnels, it can never be unseen. I would have been the other idiot wearing a tie and feigning interest in your business card requirements by appearing to take notes but actually creating an itemised list of things I would rather be doing, starting with #1. Being shot in the neck with an arrow.

Sometimes when I am in meetings, I imagine I am a robot programmed not to realise I am a robot and if the code word 'quantifiable' is mentioned, I will explode. I never do though. Other times I imagine I am a small Indian girl collecting water for my village in brightly painted clay pots.

The Jumping Frog charge relates to an event early on in my career when I made the mistake of offering a client a fixed price for a two hundred page website.

Once the design was signed off and the build completed over a three month period, the client requested that each page include a frog jumping around the screen because his wife liked frogs.

Purchasing a frog from the local pet store and filming it by holding a camera above and a cigarette lighter behind to persuade it to jump, I spent the next two weeks incorporating it into every page of the website. A few days later, the client described the addition as "very annoying" and requested it be removed and replaced with a 3D animated frog jumping onto the screen, holding a thumb up, and speaking the words "jump on down and grab a bargain." After providing a quote for this, I was informed that the amendments would be made "under the original fixed price or no payment would be made at all." The next day, their home page was replaced with a single image of a frog giving the finger and a voice bubble stating "I jump for cash, bitch."

After fifteen years in the design industry and realising the only difference between sitting in front of a computer facilitating client's requests and kneeling on the urine soaked floor of a truck stop bathroom giving five dollar blowjobs to men named Chuck, is the amount of urine on the floor, the Jumping Frog fee has evolved from insurance against post-project client suggestion to client incentive to have somebody else do it.

Regards, David.

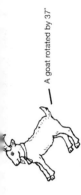

From: Robert Schaefer
Date: Monday 8 November 2010 5.09pm
To: DavidThorne
Subject: Re: Re: Re: Re: Re: Re: Artwork

You have until 10am tomorrow morning to send me the business card artwork or you will hear from my lawyer. I am sick to death of dealing with you designers. Being able to draw and dressing like a woman doesn't make you special.You've got no idea who you are dealing with.

From: DavidThorne
Date: Monday 8 November 2010 5.37pm
To: Robert Schaefer
Subject: Re: Re: Re: Re: Re: Re: Re: Artwork

Dear Bob,

That may be so, but the label "some guy who wants free shit" does not require CSI profiling and while I am no lawyer, I question whether testimony comprising entirely of "I paid an agency to provide me files, I lost the files, I now demand some guy who used to work there give me new files" would have much legal standing but best of luck with that.

I also question your dissatisfaction with the price I have quoted as I believe the original charge for your work by the agency was around eighteen hundred dollars. While the actual process would have consisted of ten minutes on iStock.com for the background, two minutes pretending to consider a typeface other than Helvetica and ten minutes putting it together, this is standard design industry practice and listed under 'Direction, Design and Build' on the invoice.

I do understand your objection to the established system of exchange of money for services though, and personally envision a utopian future where it is replaced with interpretive dance. We agree on a particular style that seeks to translate particular feelings and emotions into movement and dramatic expression in exchange for groceries or business card artwork. And we all own jetpacks.

In a moment of stupidity, I once agreed to design and build a website in exchange for yoga lessons. Contrary to what they would have you believe, you cannot actually embrace the sun as this would result in severe burns and your arms would need to be over one hundred and fifty million miles long. My favourite yoga move is the wriggly snake. Unfortunately, until I can pay my rent with mantras and expressions of emotional intonations through grand eloquent movements and wide swooshes of the arms before spinning and dropping to the floor while wearing spandex, I will need cash.

Regards, David.

From: Robert Schaefer
Date: Monday 8 November 2010 5.44pm
To: David Thorne
Subject: Re: Re: Re: Re: Re: Re: Re: Re: Artwork

Ok. Send me the completed artwork tonight with an invoice.

From: David Thorne
Date: Monday 8 November 2010 5.49pm
To: Robert Schaefer
Subject: File attached:

164

Ten reasons I probably shouldn't be alive:
Camping

I have never been a massive fan of camping. I enjoy the interesting bits like lighting fires, pitching tents and paddling in kayaks, but the bits where you sit around on fold up chairs in-between the interesting bits without access to television or a computer are boring. I have comfy chairs at home and a Keurig and pizza delivery and when I get bored I can argue on forums about things I couldn't care less about or take a hot shower.

When my parents first divorced, my father took me camping quite often. He probably felt it was important to bond during that time. We would usually camp on the banks of the River Murray. Once, while we were driving along a dirt road on our way to the river, I was being difficult about something and my father told me off, saying, "Stop talking back or you can sit outside on the roof-rack" to which I stupidly replied, "Good." Two minutes later, I was clinging to the roof-rack as the car hurtled over rough terrain and slid around dirt corners. Leaning forward, I banged on the windshield but my father turned on the wipers. A few seconds later, a bird hit me in the face. Having "ruined the camping trip", we drove to the hospital where I received stitches. On the accident report, my father wrote "skateboarding accident" and gave me twenty dollars not to say otherwise.

I realise the media has perpetuated the myth that all Australians enjoy the outback and that we all own big knives, wear dungaree shorts, and wrestle crocodiles, but this is not the case. I don't know anyone who has ever wrestled a crocodile or has the slightest inclination to do so. When Steve Irwin was stabbed in the chest while teasing a stingray that was minding its own business, I was sad for his family's loss but the suggestion of creating a 'National Steve Irwin Day' and describing him as "an ambassador for Australia" and "ecological spokesperson" left me bewildered. All he did was perpetuate the same clichés that Crocodile Dundee did in the 80's and while I am all for the tormentation of animals, I cannot recall a single instance where wrestling a stressed alligator for ten minutes instead of tranquilizing it peacefully was actually speaking for anything apart from ratings. I would like to wrestle Bindi in a muddy creek for ten minutes, rolling her around, cutting off her air supply and bending her limbs back before bounding her with rope and throwing her in the back of ute for no other reason than it would be good television.

Several years ago, I went camping with a few associates and knowing there would be times between lighting fires, pitching tents and paddling in kayaks, I thought it would be entertaining for everyone if I jumped out from behind bushes while wearing a bear suit. Renting the only 'bear' costume available, which was actually a koala, I altered it as best I could to make it look frightening by taping down the fluffy ears, adding sharp cardboard teeth and constructing two downward slanting eyebrows with electrical tape.

While everyone was sitting around the campfire, I excused myself, donned the concealed costume and leapt out yelling 'Rawr.' Moments later, I realised the screaming and falling back off chairs was not due to wearing a bear costume but the fact I was standing in the fire while wearing a bear costume made of polyester. After a two-hour drive to the nearest hospital, I underwent three weeks of skin grafting on my left leg and six months of hearing about how I ruined the camping trip. To this day, when anyone asks about the scars, I simply state "It involved a camping trip and a bear, I don't like to talk about it", which is true because I don't.

The last time I went camping in Australia, was with a group of people I didn't like - other designers from my work. I have no idea why I agreed to it but I did so at the pub after several beers and I was the only person who owned a four wheel drive vehicle with roof racks on which to place kayaks so somehow, their opinion not mine, I would be letting everyone down by not participating.

The next day we all drove to a secluded spot, four hours from Adelaide, on the banks of the Murray River. After lighting a fire and pitching tents, everyone sat around talking about work and drinking warm beer (due to the task of remembering to bring ice being left to Simon), so I decided to take a kayak for a paddle to get away from them. I changed into boardshorts, grabbed my iPhone, and paddled off down the river towards a bend where I would not be seen by the others.

Finding that the current was quite strong and realising I would have to paddle back against it, I rounded the bend, pulled up against a dead tree branch sticking out of the water, and tied my kayak to it using the drawstring from my boardshorts.

Removing my shirt and lying back to enjoy the warmth of the sun, I put in my earphones and fell asleep listening to Lil' Jon and The Eastside Boyz yelling about "throwin' stuff up."

Approximately five hours later, I woke up. Looking down, I discovered my entire body covered by several hundred mosquitos. Sitting up quickly to brush madly at my torso and legs, the iPhone that had been laying on my chest went flying, ripping the earbuds from my ears, and disappeared beneath the algae laden surface.

Looking around, I also discovered that the tree branch I had secured the kayak to with my drawstring, rotten from years of being waterlogged, had snapped off and was now trailing behind my kayak which had drifted with the current down the river. Having no idea how far away I was from camp but knowing that I had better make it back before nightfall, I began paddling madly back up the river, pausing every few minutes to scratch at the thousands of bites.

I read on a website forum somewhere that if a mosquito is on your arm and you pull the skin tight, the mosquito can't get its beak (or whatever its pointy thing is called) out, so it just keeps sucking until it pops. I have tried this and it is rubbish. People need to stop making up things on the internet. (I just looked up mosquitos on Wikipedia and apparently the pointy bit is called the Proboscis. Which just means nose. Which is worse somehow.) Once, when I was dragged to a sporting event, I saw a mosquito on the neck of the guy in front of me and, thinking he would thank me, I slapped it and the man spun around and punched me in the head. Shocked, I said, "there was a mosquito on your neck." I held out my hand to show him and, looking confused, he said "I don't want it."

An hour later it was dark. I'm not talking about the kind of dark you get in cities where there is usually a vague glow from lights being reflected by clouds or pollution, or even the kind of dark where you can kind of navigate by moonlight, this was the kind of dark where the term 'pitch' is appropriate. I could no longer tell where I was steering the kayak or even if I was heading up the river or down. Using my lighter only lit up about a metre around me making the darkness beyond seem darker. I have read somewhere that sailors can navigate by the stars but even when told that a certain structure of stars is a ram or horse-man with a bow and arrow, I fail to see it. With no city light reflection, clouds or moon, the entire sky was filled with stars. Except for a black spot without stars directly ahead of me which I aimed for - figuring it was probably another dead tree sticking out of the water to which I could at least secure my kayak and wait out the night.

I was about half way to the object when my kayak scraped, and then wedged against something beneath it. Figuring I must have struck a shallow area near shore, I tried to release the kayak by paddling backwards and even pushing my paddle down like a gondola driver but it would not come free.

Not knowing how far from the shore I was or even its direction or what the object ahead of me was, I did not for a second consider stepping out into the water.

The first time I had gone camping on the river many years prior, I had let my feet dangle in the water off the side of a jetty and not two minutes had gone by before I felt a sharp pain in my toe, pulled my foot out of the water, and found a turtle the size of a dinner plate attached and unwilling to let go of its meal. I had to club it to death with a beer bottle.

Having no option but to wait until the light of morning, I curled up in the kayak and a few hours later, fell asleep to sounds of waves lapping against the side and the whine of mosquitos attempting to find an area not already bitten.

I awoke at first light to the cries of "Hello? Are you alright?" and "he looks like he has a million mosquito bites all over him" coming from quite close. I sat up to discover that the object I had been heading for the night before was a houseboat moored to the side of the river and was only about four kayak lengths away. An elderly couple stood on the deck drinking coffee looking at me. My first reaction was to ask, "where am I?" and the man replied, "In a kayak."

After accepting the kind offer of a cup of coffee and calamine lotion from Joyce and Richard, and being told that Pelican Point was "approximately an hour up river", I set off and arrived at camp several hours later due to Joyce and Richard's wildly inaccurate approximations, to find everyone packing and quite pissed off that nobody else got to have a turn in the kayak. No search party had been sent out and two people thought I had been in my tent the whole time because I "never join in with group activities."

On the four hour angry drive back, I made everyone to listen to Lil' Jon and The Eastside Boyz yelling about 'throwin' stuff up' on loop.

Simon giving oral sex to a model of a 19th century clipper.

The annoying horn thing in the grill procedure

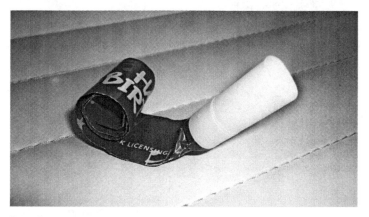

Step 1

Purchase one of those horn things that roll out when you blow into them. You have to get the ones that make a loud "brawwww" sound, not the stupid ones that you blow into and they are just a tube that makes no noise. This time around, I accidently bought the kind that don't make the noise but as there is no sound in the book, I will just pretend that the one shown above is the kind that makes the noise. If you are going to carry on about the availability of the ones that make the noise, a plastic whistle will do. It's really not that complicated.

To describe the horn in the grill procedure, I probably could have just said "You hide a horn/whistle in the grill" but cutting things up, rolling poster-putty and taking photographs, made it look like I was busy. During the process, My partner Holly asked if I wanted to go with her to Target to buy a shoe cupboard but, unfortunately, the horn/whistle/grill photographs weren't going to take themselves.

Step 2

Cut the bit off that rolls out when you blow into the horn. You can throw that bit away unless you have another project or something you are working on that requires it.

Step 3

Roll a blob of poster-putty around the horn. I had originally written the product name Blutac® in place of poster-putty but Americans have different names for things so I changed it to Plasticine but then I wasn't sure if that was even a real word so I wrote poster-putty instead.

Step 3

Squeeze the blob encircled horn/whistle, with the end you blow into facing outwards, into the front grill of a car belonging to somebody that has annoyed you / likes Nickelback.

Step 4

Check the horn is not visible. When the driver of the vehicle reaches a speed of around fifty, air flowing into the horn opening will cause it to make the noise until the vehicle slows down. When they get out to check where the noise is coming from, it will have stopped.

F26-A

Date 10 /AUG/ 2011	Date of offense 10 AUG 2011

Name of person filing F26-A SIMON DEMPSEY

Name/s of person/s involved DAVID THORNE

Complaint type ☑ Internal ☐ External ☐ Other:

Description   Ref: ☑ Formal ☐ Med ☑ Class 1 ☐ Class 2

I TOOK MY CAR TO A MECHANIC TODAY
BECAUSE IT WAS MAKING A NOISE WHEN
I DROVE IT AND THE MECHANIC FOUND A
HORN STUCK IN THE GRILL WITH PLAYDOH.
HIDDEN. I KNOW IT WAS DAVID THORNE
BECAUSE WHO ELSE WOULD DO IT?

Action Requested ☑ Disciplinary ☐ Mediation ☐ Other:

Signature   10 AUG/ 2011

Office Use Only

Ref ☒ F26-A ☐ F26-B   Lodged: ☒ Y ☐ N

F26-B Attached ☐ Y ☒ N   Date AUG 10 2011

RECEIVED

Girls like telephones and apps. It isn't rocket science.

I wasn't expecting Kevin to actually send the client a proof but it will be interesting to see how this pans out.

Despite the fact that most agency account reps have never worked in, or have the vaguest idea about, the industry they represent, I like working with Kevin for exactly this reason.

In the past year, he has asked me to courier him "a portable document disk", promised a client a new logo in exchange for 50% off the price of laying floor boards in his home, and once fell asleep during a client meeting. When I startled him awake by nudging him, he yelled "the sprinklers are on" but refused to go into further detail.

I have only ever seen Kevin seriously lose his temper once. He was in a really bad mood about something one day and I asked him if he had a piece of paper and a pen. He snapped back "Do I look like the fucking stationery cupboard?" so I said "No, the stationary cupboard is half your age and useful" and he replied "Oh really, can the stationary cupboard do this?" then picked up my iPhone and dropped it in my coffee before storming out. The next day, I arrived at work to find a ream of paper, about twenty pens, and a thirty dollar replacement phone with a twenty dollar recharge card on my desk.

Also, despite having almost no idea what I am doing, part of my job role is maintaining the website - which somehow turned into maintaining the network - and progressed to fixing everyone's computer. Usually I welcome the break from real work, pretend there is an actual problem with the computer, and sit browsing at their web history for an hour or so.

While Simon's web history consists almost entirely of porn, Kevin's web history includes only: home auto maintenance, paving, caravaning tips, and for some strange reason, mermaids.

From: Kevin Eastwood
Date: Thursday 19 January 2012 10.04am
To: David Thorne
Subject: Kotex artwork

Hi David,

I just tried emailing Jodie but got an auto responder that she is away. The client was happy with the last magazine ad layout and wants to place another in the February issue. Same info but different image. I said I would get a proof to them by tomorrow. Can you have a look at this for me?

Kevin

....

From: David Thorne
Date: Thursday 19 January 2012 10.32am
To: Kevin Eastwood
Subject: Re: Kotex artwork

Hello Kevin,

Jodie is currently away on stress leave but will be returning on the 23rd. Workload related stress is a leading cause of poor office productivity and a daily schedule of harvesting Farmville crops while eating cake and emailing people images of a cat wearing a tie saying "I need everyone to stay late tonight, we really need to catch that red dot" apparently falls under this description.

While I would love to help you out, unfortunately I am unable to make amendments to Jodie's projects in her absence. This is partly due to not being the designer who undertook the brief, research, direction and development of the project, and partly due to Jodie password-protecting her computer after I changed her open Facebook page status to "Renting the Die Hard quadrilogy tonight. Yippee kayak, motherfuckers" while she was at a funeral.

In my defence, I thought she said she was going to a "Food Mall." Just last week Mellisa stated there was cake in the kitchen and I heard a popping noise as air entered the vacuum Jodie's mass had occupied at her desk a nanosecond before.

Though I know her password, (it is always her cat's name), there is little point using it. As Jodie has modeled her filing system on the Mandelbrot Set, with files named qwedqwyer.fmx and asdasydfg.psd several thousand folders deep, she will probably be back at work well

Margin note:

Once, while copying a file to Jodie's desktop as she stood watching and scowling that someone would dare touch her computer, I inadvertantly hovered the mouse over the 'Arrange by Date' menu item and was block-tackled off the chair. For a fat girl, she can move suprisingly fast.

174

before I manage to locate the file. I can leave a sticky note on her desk though if that helps.

Regards, David.

From: Kevin Eastwood
Date: Thursday 19 January 2012 10.46am
To: David Thorne
Subject: Re: Re: Kotex artwork

Not really. You don't have to search for the file it is 0396_kotex_click_advert_01.pdf. It has the black panel at the bottom with the Kotex logo and info and the picture of the girls at the beach splashing each other. The picture and the quote just needs to be changed, keep the rest. I fully realize Jodie worked on the account but when she is away other designers should have access to the files If someone needs them. Standard operating procedure. I guess having some kind of system in this place is too much to hope for.

Kevin

From: David Thorne
Date: Thursday 19 January 2012 11.01am
To: Kevin Eastwood
Subject: Re: Re: Re: Kotex artwork

Kevin,

We do have some kind of system and it is entirely hope based. Standard operating procedures consist of hoping nobody notices, hoping someone else gets blamed, and hoping account managers make promises only after checking the availability of sources to fulfill those promises.

Last month, while a file was in pre-press after a two day photo-shoot featuring five babies for a Kimberly Clarke advertisement and a week of design, you asked if it was too late to "make the text bigger and one of the babies an Asian."

If you expect me to make amendments to the Kotex layout, I am hoping that you have either a budget allocated for sourcing a replacement image that represents the confidence and resulting lifestyle benefits gained by using a particular brand of tampon, or have an existing 'rights free' replacement image in mind.

Regards, David.

From: Kevin Eastwood
Date: Thursday 19 January 2012 11.09am
To: David Thorne
Subject: Re: Re: Re: Re: Kotex artwork

Budget for what? It is one photo change. It really isn't that complicated. Instead of girls at the beach, just change it to girls riding bikes or something and change the quote to something about being confident.

....

From: David Thorne
Date: Thursday 19 January 2012 12.16pm
To: Kevin Eastwood
Subject: Requested amendment.

Attached file 0396_kotex_click_advert_01B.pdf

Simon giving oral sex to a motorbike.

From: Kevin Eastwood
Date: Thursday 19 January 2012 12.33pm
To: David Thorne
Subject: Re: Requested amendment.

Ok. The photo is nice but it doesn't have anything to do with tampons and the copy doesn't make any sense. You cant even tell if it is a girl or guy and I didn't say motorbikes.

I said bikes. If it was a cute girl smiling and hugging a guy on the back of a moped or something that might work but not doing jumps.

....

From: David Thorne
Date: Thursday 19 January 2012 12.51pm
To: Kevin Eastwood
Subject: Re: Re: Requested amendment.

Attached file 0396_kotex_click_advert_01C.pdf

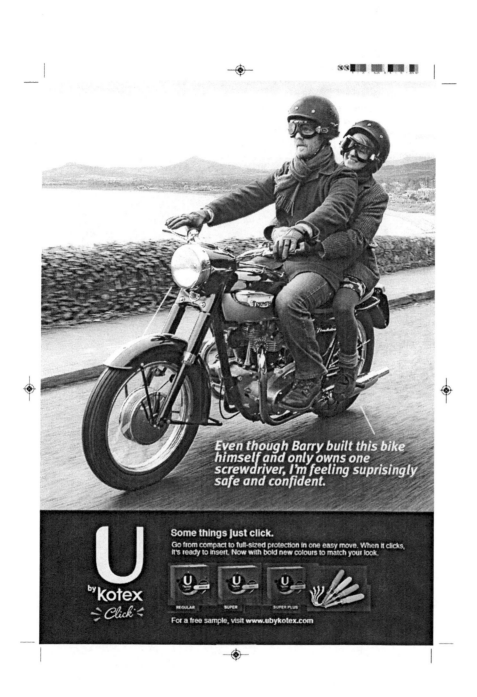

Even though Barry built this bike himself and only owns one screwdriver, I'm feeling suprisingly safe and confident.

From: Kevin Eastwood
Date: Thursday 19 January 2012 1.19pm
To: David Thorne
Subject: Re: Re: Re: Requested amendment.

I liked the first one better. That's not a moped and I meant parked or something not riding. How is that image meant to appeal to anyone? They look like idiots and the bike is too old. Girls like modern technology like telephones and apps. It isn't rocket science.

From: David Thorne
Date: Thursday 19 January 2012 1.46pm
To: Kevin Eastwood
Subject: Re: Re: Re: Re: Requested amendment.

Attached file 0396_kotex_click_advert_01D.pdf

From: Kevin Eastwood
Date: Thursday 19 January 2012 2.46pm
To: David Thorne
Subject: Re: Re: Re: Re: Re: Requested amendment.

I will just send them the first one of the girl doing a jump and get back to you if they have changes. Thanks.

....

From: David Thorne
Date: Thursday 19 January 2012 2.51pm
To: Kevin Eastwood
Subject: Re: Re: Re: Re: Re: Re: Requested amendment.

No problem. You may want to CC Jodie in on that as I intend to be away next week.

....

From: Kevin Eastwood
Date: Thursday 19 January 2012 2.57pm
To: David Thorne
Subject: Re: Re: Re: Re: Re: Re: Re: Requested amendment.

Will do.

They're fucking shooting at us! They have already killed Barry. Quick, drop down and change direction!

Posting fake news articles after guessing Holly's password

Aliens Cure Pennsylvanian Woman's Arthritis
August 13 2011

The small town of Warren, Pennsylvania, which lies near Lake Erie on the edge of Allegheny National Forest, is quickly becoming the latest hotspot for those in search of close encounters with alien life. Warren is usually a fairly quiet town, large enough to have a high school, but small enough for the locals to notice when changes occur. Most recently, the heightened military activity following four reports in as many months of strange sightings, and one report of abduction.

Joy Davies, 62, is not the kind of person you would usually expect to say "aliens took me." She enjoys walking her dog Ben, volunteers on weekends at the Goodwill, and can be seen most days in her garden wielding a trowel and wearing a broad rimmed straw hat. Her husband Jack died last year after a lengthy bout with pneumonia. Every evening, Mrs. Davies takes Ben for a walk along the trail in the woods behind her house. On August 2nd, Mrs. Davies states that as she walked around the bend of the trail, only a few minutes into the walk, she was taken by aliens. "I wasn't scared at all," she stated, "they were very polite and I felt safe the whole time. I was more worried about telling anybody as I thought I would be called nutty. Everyone has been very nice about it though." Mrs. Davies described the aliens as the size of children, very pale and with no hair. "They were smiling and one of them told me not to be afraid without speaking," she said. She then went on to describe the ship as "More like a peanut shape than like the flying saucers you see in those action movies, and white with a soft blue glow beneath it lighting the area. I don't remember entering the ship but I knew I was inside because the walls were curved and the blue light was underneath me. Ben was next to me and one of the aliens was scratching behind his ears, which he likes. A tiny bright blue light like a star, but about the size of a snowflake, appeared above me and slowly floated down so I held out my hand to catch it and when it touched my hand I remember laughing. The next thing I remember is standing on the path facing my house. One of the aliens was holding my hand. When he let go and turned back down the path, I don't know why I didn't turn to watch, but instead I just walked back to the house with Ben and made a cup of tea.

I then went to bed because somehow four hours had passed and it was late." While Mrs. Davies has "no idea why it happened," she believes what occurred that evening cured her arthritis. "Up until that night I suffered from arthritis really bad, especially in my hands and arms, and took pills daily. Now I haven't got it at all and haven't taken a single pill since. I played tennis for the first time in several years with my friend Cathy last week and can knit again. Ben seems more frisky, too."

Prior to Joy's alleged encounter, four different people had reported seeing strange lights in the area. Michael Smith, 58, stated that he had seen a white blob around 10pm a few weeks earlier above the tree line of his property before it "flashed brighter and then just disappeared." Three similar sightings have been reported since April and last week, government officials sealed off a section of the forest for three days. "There were trucks and soldiers," said local shop owner Carol Banks, "they just drove into the forest and three days later they drove out. We weren't told anything and nobody bought anything."

While no reason apart from "standard training exercises" has been given for the heightened military activity, Warren is a small town and gossip travels quickly. As Mrs. Davies works in her garden for as long as she wants "now that the arthritis is gone," neighbors stop to say hello and speculate about what may have been under the tarp on the back of the third truck.

Family Dog Rescues 6-year-old From Raging River
August 18 2011

On August 17, Tom and Marie Morgan of Ridgefield, Washington were walking along the edge of a tributary of the Lewis River with their six year-old daughter Taylor and family dog Maggie. The river was in full flow due to recent heavy rains. As Taylor ran forward to throw a rock into the river, the bank collapsed and, falling into the rushing torrent, Taylor was quickly swept away.

"I couldn't keep up with her," said her father, "the water was too quick." I was running as fast as I could along the edge when Maggie bolted past me for about 30 yards and then leaped into the river. I lost sight of both of them for a second and then I saw Maggie with Taylor's jacket collar in her mouth trying to swim towards the bank.

The river took them down about another hundred yards before Maggie was able to reach the bank. Even though they went under a few times she didn't let go once. If it hadn't been for Maggie, we would have lost our daughter."

An eyewitness who was jogging nearby when the incident happened said, "The dog jumped about 12 feet out into the river just in front of the child. They both went under and when they came up the dog had her jacket in its mouth and was dragging her to the bank. The dad ran into the water's edge and grabbed the other side of the child's jacket and they both dragged her up onto the grass. I have never seen anything like it."

Sergeant Michael Brodie of the local police department said that in twenty years on the force he had not seen anything like it either. "I have never heard of a dog jumping into a river to save a child before. The family is very lucky to own a dog with this degree of devotion. When I took the report at the family's home, the dog sat there looking back and forth between me and Taylor and I could sense something extremely unusual between them." Taylor's father Tom says that it is not the first time Maggie has displayed an unusual degree of devotion towards Taylor. "Maggie never lets her out of her sight. About two years ago she rushed into the house, breaking the screen, barking as if she had gone crazy. She is usually very gentle and quiet. When my wife and I rushed to see what was happening she ran out into the yard where we found Taylor lying on the grass having trouble breathing. She had been stung on the neck and is highly allergic to bees." When Taylor was younger and first walking, Maggie would move toys out of her path and always sleeps just outside her bedroom door as if on guard." When asked about her river rescue, Taylor responded "Maggie loves me."

Today, the Morgan family received notice that Maggie has been nominated for a Commendation of Bravery by the police department. Unfortunately, the medal may have to be given posthumously.
"We found out last month that Maggie has been diagnosed with Hemangiosarcoma cancer and will not be with us in a few months; we haven't told Taylor yet as she will be devastated. It will be the hardest thing we have ever had to do. The two have an inseparable bond that is based on real love. We owe our daughter's life to her."

Hello, my name is Christopher and my left breast is named Carl.

The Morton Report Apologises For Fabricated Stories
August 19 2011 Posted by the editor

Over the last week, articles concerning aliens and a dog named Maggie rescuing a 6-year-old child were posted on The Morton Report under the guise of being real stories. The validity of the articles was not initially questioned as it was posted under the name of one our columnists. The poster, David Thorne, gained access to the columnist's account and posted under her name.

The article about Maggie, which ended with the dog having cancer, garnered over 40,000 hits within a 24 hour period and resulted in many readers leaving comments expressing how upset they were by the dog's medical condition. Many said they were 'deeply touched' by the article and felt they had been lifted up with a story of love and hope only to be hit with the heart-breaking ending. Hundreds of messages of hope were left for the 'parents'.

Speaking to Thorne via email, he stated "Readers received a Hallmark moment for free. Those upset by Maggie's condition can take solace in the fact that she doesn't actually have cancer." In fact, Maggie does not exist. While the location in the article is real, 6-year-old Taylor, the parents and the dog are fictitious characters constructed by Thorne for, it appears, no other purpose than "I was bored at work. Your issue should probably be with my employer for failing to provide a stimulating work environment."

We apologise for any concern the fabrications may have caused. The Morton Report has a strong stance on unsourced material and does not condone the posting of fabricated articles. As such, The Morton Report has taken steps to ensure this does not re-occur.

— Wait. What?

Hello, I hope you are enjoying the book so far. It is a little disjointed but I liked the story about the Nacho soup. It gets worse from here on in but keep going. I would love to join you but Pokey and I have a different adventure planned for today so we will stay here. I slipped him Rohypnol a few minutes ago and when he is out, I'm going to dress him as an Asian schoolgirl and

Ten reasons I probably shouldn't be alive:
The tree-house

When I was about ten, I decided to build a tree-house after reading a book called *The Swiss Family Robinson* in which a family, the Robinson's, are shipwrecked and decide to live in a tree.

Our neighbour, a rarely seen widower named Mr Anderson, owned a fenced-in quarter acre block with a large shed at the back of the property. Figuring Mr Anderson would never notice, I removed the planks from the fence behind his shed, using a claw-hammer that I found in his shed.

Using the planks to construct the frame and floor of my tree-house, I discovered I needed more planks. Removing several more from his fence, I realised that Mr Anderson would be able to see they were missing if he looked at the right angle so I covered the gap with a sheet and secured it in place with tape. Completing construction a few hours later, I spent the rest of the day furnishing and painting the interior of what was, essentially, a collection of planks balanced precariously on top of each other.

That evening, after my parents had returned from a marriage counselling session and turned in early, I decided to sneak out and sleep in my tree-house. Taking a pillow, blanket, flashlight and snacks with me, I had just settled in for the night when a light breeze caused the walls and roof of the tree-house to collapse - pinning me to the floor. The only part of me that wasn't covered was my face, leaving me staring upwards as it started to rain.

Unable to call out or move due to the crushing weight, I remained there the entire night, falling asleep at one point but waking when it started to rain harder, before finally being rescued the next morning when Mr Anderson let his cat out and heard my soft cries for help.

While I was at the hospital with two fractured ribs and collapsed lung, Mr Anderson took back his planks.

THE WALKING DEAD

Margin note:

When the first book was released, a bald guy named Brian Sendelbach sued me for using an image he drew.

When I sent him a message saying "it was one page of a 368 page book, I am happy to remove it or give you credit and a link on my website." He wrote back "Fuck you."

I then emailed Brian using a fake email address and name saying, "Hey, did you know David Thorne used one of your drawings in his book? You should sue that bitch" and he replied, "Already on it. Lol. Getting 25,000 bucks! Gonna buy a Jeep."

189

People don't wear Spandex™ doing yoga, that's jazzercise

Whoever came up with the phrase "Hell is other people" probably worked in a design agency... no, I just googled it, apparently it was some french guy with a girls name who never worked in a design agency. If Jean-Paul Sartre had worked in our design agency, he wouldn't have lasted a week. Mainly because he doesn't have a background in design.

Surprising as it may seem, I am not a huge fan of time spent with co-workers. Mainly because it usually means being at work and I am a huge fan of not being at work. When I do attend, I spend the whole day coming up with an excuse not to be there the next day so really it is just time that would be better spent on a hobby or something.

Occasionally, I am expected to spend time with co-workers outside of office hours. Last year, it was three days on a houseboat stuck on a sandbar. The year before that, Mike organised a camping trip to a lake he had visited when he was a child. After purchasing kayaks and tents, renting a trailer and driving for eight hours, we arrived to find the town abandoned, due to the lake drying up several years prior, so we drove back. I did get to poke a lizard with a stick though, so it was not a complete waste of time.

I was told once that team building tasks create a balanced working environment. It would need to be on some kind of fulcrum and if you picked up a stapler from one end you would need to replace it with something of equal weight. Probably a calculator and two pens. When someone left for lunch each day, you would need to sit something in their chair and be able to shift it on their return. Some kind of pulley system would probably be needed.

Also, to placate Mike should he ever discover this article, I have used his favourite photo from what he calls his 'icon series.' He made me spend two hours photoshopping out his wrinkles and making his hair "more like David Duchovny's."

From: Mike Campbell
Date: Monday 14 March 2011 9.06am
To: All Staff
Subject: Staff weekend

Kevin and I had a meeting on Friday to discuss doing one of those staff team building weekends. It's tax deductible and we can get a package deal with one near the river that looks nice with activities like yoga, canoeing, talent night, hiking and orienteering. It's a 3 hour drive so if we leave Friday lunch time, we will get there before 4pm. The plan is to lock in the 25th to the 27th of this month so can everyone check their schedules and confirm these dates with Mellisa please?

Mike

....

From: David Thorne
Date: Monday 14 March 2011 9.34am
To: Mike Campbell
Subject: Re: Staff weekend

Dear Mike,

Although I am usually the first to embrace any excuse for absence from the workplace, my absence usually involves a direct correlation to the absence of people I work with. Spending several hours in a vehicle to participate in activities that involve being sweaty, wet, judged and then lost together, sounds pretty much the same as a normal week in the office. Will we be paid to attend and what is the difference between hiking and orienteering?

Regards, David.

....

From: Mike Campbell
Date: Monday 14 March 2011 10.04am
To: David Thorne
Subject: Re: Re: Staff weekend

One is where you walk around and the other is where you have a compass. The point isn't what the activities are, its that we do them together as a team. I should have known you would be the first one to complain. Everybody else had a good time last year on the houseboat.

From: David Thorne
Date: Monday 14 March 2011 11.22am
To: Mike Campbell
Subject: Re: Re: Re: Staff weekend

Dear Mike,

When did I indicate that I had anything other than a good time aboard the houseboat last year? I am the last to complain about anything. If I were on a television game show where points were awarded for complaining, my only complaint would be participating in a show that is clearly beyond my means of winning. At the end of the show, I would thank the host and say I had a wonderful time anyway.

My favourite part was when we were stuck on a sandbar for three days. Unable to radio for help due to your hair dryer usage draining the reserve batteries, you claimed yourself captain and ordered me to swim ashore in search of a tall tree to climb with the hope of gaining mobile phone reception. It is not mutiny if the captain cannot provide sufficient evidence to support his title, and you refused to accept my title of Grand Admiral Emperor King of Everything the next day.

My second favourite part of the trip was when you drank our entire week's alcohol supply on the first afternoon, fell from the bow, and yelled at me for not diving in to rescue you. In my defence, I was wearing new shoes and did give the area a quick visual check for anything of sufficient buoyancy to cast to you. Failing that, I felt the next best thing would be the ability to later provide an accurate eye-witness account. I would have left out the bits where you screamed, "Something touched my leg" and "Not like this. Not like this."

Just this morning I was sitting here thinking, while nodding randomly to portray interest in Jodie's dilemma regarding missing Farmville credits and watching Simon pick his nose and wipe it under his desk, that the one thing missing in my life is a greater percentage of time spent with these people.

If I take a compass with me on the hike does that mean I can skip the orienteering? This would leave me with only yoga, canoeing and talent night to avoid participating in.

Regards, David.

From: Mike Campbell
Date: Monday 14 March 2011 11.46am
To: David Thorne
Subject: Re: Re: Re: Re: Staff weekend

It wasn't 3 days. It was less than an hour. What is the point of you even going this year if you are not going to participate in TEAM activities??

From: David Thorne
Date: Monday 14 March 2011 1.09pm
To: Mike Campbell
Subject: Re: Re: Re: Re: Re: Staff weekend

Dear Mike,

My point exactly. It might be interesting to see what talents the staff comes up with for talent night though. I have been working here for a year and haven't seen any. Yoga is out of the question; seeing Kevin and Simon clad in Spandex, kicking and rolling around on the floor like a couple of neon walruses engaged in a territorial dispute, is probably a breach of Occupational Health & Safety regulations.

I'm fine with canoeing though. As long as I can sit in the back and pretend to paddle only when the person in the front turns around to complain about me not paddling; it might be a nice break from avoiding activities. If it is one of those little single-person kayaks, my non-paddling will have the added benefit of failing to keep up with the group. As you all pass around a bend in the river, I will have the opportunity, should I decide to take it, to roll the kayak and drown.

Also, what are the sleeping arrangements? I won't share with Simon again after the last time. I was unable to sleep due to his controlled breathing and rustling. It was around 3am before I realised why he had placed the mini hair-conditioner bottle from the hotel bathroom on his side table and what the clicking and squeezing sounds were.

I have attached a diagram indicating proposed travel, sleeping and activity arrangements. I am A, everyone else is B, and C is a lockable door. Will we be paid to attend?

Regards, David.

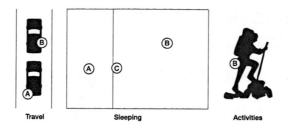

Travel   Sleeping   Activities

From: Mike Campbell
Date: Monday 14 March 2011 1.18pm
To: David Thorne
Subject: Re: Re: Re: Re: Re: Re: Staff weekend

You don't wear spandex, you wear loose clothing. And no you don't get paid to go on a staff weekend trip. What a stupid question. Not counting food and travel, it costs us $3200 just to stay there and Mellisa has budgeted another $500 for alcohol.

From: Mellisa Peters
Date: Monday 14 March 2011 2.26pm
To: David Thorne
Subject: Hey

Hi, are you coming to the staff weekend event on the 25th?

From: David Thorne
Date: Monday 14 March 2011 2.41pm
To: Mellisa Peters
Subject: Re: Hey

Looking forward to it. On talent night, I'm going to perform a disappearing act with a bottle of scotch and a kayak. You?

From: Mellisa Peters
Date: Monday 14 March 2011 2.53pm
To: David Thorne
Subject: Re: Re: Hey

I don't know yet. Probably a dance or something.

David and his best friends go shopping

Margin note:

Years ago, while at a shopping mall, I noticed that a lot of people were looking at my shoes as I walked past. I figured they were impressed with my new G-star sneakers. While waiting for a elevator, a girl approached and quietly pointed out that the underpants I had worn the day before, and inadvertently left in my jeans, had worked their way down one leg and were hanging out the bottom like a flag. I told her that they were not mine before realising that having another man's underpants hanging out the bottom of my jeans was worse so quickly added "no, sorry that was a lie, they are my underpants." After an awkward pause, I asked her out but she said no.

There's nothing wrong with my design, it just needs to be more branded.

Martin's staff profile includes the following bio which I think Martin may have written himself:

"Martin has a degree in fine arts and is a Windows expert. If you have a computer problem, Martin is your man. When he is not solving problems that noone else can at work, he enjoys listening to live jazz, fishing and playing with his dog Tolkien."

Martin is also an aspiring graphic designer. His style can be likened to jazz in that only people like Martin think it is any good.

Two weeks ago, I was commissioned by the company Martin works for to redesign their marketing materials.

As the designer of their current brochure (shown right), Martin took the news surprisingly hard. While I do commend anyone expressing creativity with whatever tools they have available, owning copies of Photoshop and InDesign does not make you a graphic designer.

I have owned a hammer for years but that doesn't mean I can build a house. I would give it a go but I am not stupid enough to think it would be pleasant to look at or up to code. I did build a squirrel house recently though. It took me an entire week. two weeks later it rained and all the wood bowed and the nails popped out. I saw it collapse the other day and had to lift the roof to free a rather pissed squirrel.

From: Martin Buchanan
Date: Friday 8 Mar 2013 10.06am
To: David Thorne
Subject: Brochure

Hello. Louise asked me to send you the brochure files. I'm quite excited to see what changes we are making. Do you want the indesign files or just the text and images? If you are just changing the images I could do that here if you wanted. I know how to use Indesign.

From: David Thorne
Date: Friday 8 Mar 2013 10.13am
To: Martin Buchanan
Subject: Re: Brochure

Dear Martin,

Thank you for your email. While I appreciate the offer, I will not require any existing components for the redesign.

Regards, David.

From: Martin Buchanan
Date: Friday 8 Mar 2013 10.25am
To: David Thorne
Subject: Re: Re: Brochure

Are you going to just make it more branded or redraw everything? That seems like it would take a long time when I already have the files. Are you changing how things look? I don't think it needs a big change just the photos on the back need updating and the new web address. Do you want me to copy and paste the text and the images into an email for your changes or do want to tell me what changes to make and I make them?

From: David Thorne
Date: Friday 8 Mar 2013 10.37am
To: Martin Buchanan
Subject: Re: Re: Re: Brochure

Hello Martin,

Your enthusiasm is commendable but I do not require any files from you at this stage. I have been commissioned to redesign the complete suite of marketing materials and this includes the brochure. If for some reason I do decide to use any of the existing graphic components, a quick search on Google for 'clipart of man holding clipboard' and 'blue wiggly line for no apparent reason' should suffice.

Regards, David.

....

From: Martin Buchanan
Date: Friday 8 Mar 2013 10.51am
To: David Thorne
Subject: Re: Re: Re: Re: Brochure

The blue line represents growth, like on the stock market. There's nothing wrong with the current design, it just needs to be more branded. If you add more brand without changing the design and update the photos it will be perfect. Do you want me to send you the logo? Are you changing the text?

....

From: David Thorne
Date: Friday 8 Mar 2013 10.58am
To: Martin Buchanan
Subject: Re: Re: Re: Re: Re: Brochure

Hello Martin,

While I will be using segments of the current text, primarily the words 'and' and 'it', the majority will be rewritten and the logo, which appears to have been created by someone with severe Apophenia, needs to be redrawn in a higher resolution than the current 6x8 pixels.

Regards, David.

....

From: Martin Buchanan
Date: Friday 8 Mar 2013 11.18am
To: David Thorne
Subject: Re: Re: Re: Re: Re: Re: Brochure

No it doesn't. What bits are you changing? You should just send the text changes to me and I will make them on the files. It doesn't make sense to change how the brochure looks too much. We shouldn't be changing it at all, it's just a waste of money. We've still got four boxes of the current ones left downstairs. It would make more sense to print stickers and stick them over the old web address on the back. I designed that brochure and it has had a lot of good feedback.

From: David Thorne
Date: Friday 8 Mar 2013 11.36am
To: Martin Buchanan
Subject: Re: Re: Re: Re: Re: Re: Re: Brochure

Hello Martin,

Your mother stating "That's nice dear" probably falls under the label of encouragement rather than feedback.

I often tell my offspring that he is talented despite the artwork on our refrigerator clearly illustrating the opposite. I commended him last week on an excellent representation of an octopus only to find out that it was meant to be a car. Unfortunately, confidence through encouragement does not automatically equate to capability. If I were to use my offspring's artwork on a brochure for the Ford Motor Company, feedback comprising of "Is that a fucking octopus?" would be far more likely than "This will sell a lot of cars, just add some clipart of a man holding a clipboard and a blue wiggly line and it's good to go."

While some people might describe the current brochure as sophisticated, message driven, and on-brand, those people should be reminded that sarcasm is the lowest form of wit.

As a designer, I do understand attachment to something you have created and that other people's opinions are merely hurdles constructed of inanity, but as every component of a company's marketing materials define that company's brand message, which in this instance appears to be "look at how many different typefaces our computer has", the decision to hide them in the basement was probably a wise one.

Regards, David.

From: Martin Buchanan
Date: Friday 8 Mar 2013 11.57am
To: David Thorne
Subject: Re: Re: Re: Re: Re: Re: Re: Re: Brochure

They're not hidden, they're on a shelf. Obviously you're going to say my design isn't very good so you can justify charging to redesign it. Everyone who has seen the current brochure has said it is amazing. Ive got a degree in fine arts and I've done an advanced course in Adobe. I probably know more indesign than you do. Art is subjective. I branded it to appeal to our customers, they don't want modern looking things.

From: David Thorne
Date: Friday 8 Mar 2013 12.19pm
To: Martin Buchanan
Subject: Re: Re: Re: Re: Re: Re: Re: Re: Re: Brochure

Hello Martin,

The company you work for sells water heaters. I might be missing something but I fail to understand how stock market graphs and rainbow gradient backgrounds relate to warm showers.

While art is certainly subjective, it has also been said that art is a tryst, for in the joy of it, maker and beholder meet. Unfortunately, in this case, the tryst would be the emotional-connection equivalent of a quick handjob in a K-mart toilet from a middle-aged shelf-stacker named Rhonda in exchange for half a packet of Marlboro Menthol lights.

That's not to say the current design is completely without its merits. Running multi-coloured drop-shadowed type to the very edges has effectively removed the need to fill in all that annoying negative space with more clipart and, having chosen to ignore the corporate colour, using every other colour was an interesting approach. When Louise first handed me the brochure, I thought she was inviting me to a rave.

If nothing else, your style is certainly unique. During my twenty-odd years of working with professionals in the design industry, I can honestly say I have never seen anything quite like it. Once the redesign is completed, I am happy to send you a proof following pre-press and you are welcome to provide any suggestions you may have at that time.

Regards, David.

···

From: Martin Buchanan
Date: Friday 8 Mar 2013 1.08pm
To: David Thorne
Subject: Re: Re: Re: Re: Re: Re: Re: Re: Re: Re: Brochure

Don't bother sending me a proof. I'm not going to be here next week and I'm not interested in seeing it or reading any more of your bullshit anyway. I'm busy organizing a fishing trip and leave tonight. Convincing people they need to redesign things when there is nothing wrong with what they have so you can make some quick cash just makes you a con artist. I've got more talent in my little finger than you have in your whole body. Dropshadows lift the type off the page as if they are 3D. You probably don't even know how to do them. Have fun redoing the whole brochure without any files. While you're sitting at your desk redrawing everything next week, I will be relaxing in a chair with my new Shimano rod and laughing.

....

From: Louise Brown
Date: Friday 8 Mar 2013 3.22pm
To: David Thorne
Subject: Files

Hi David,

Just wondering if you received the brochure files. We have the photographer coming in on Monday so can hopefully get product shots to you mid week. Have a great weekend.

Louise.

....

From: David Thorne
Date: Friday 8 Mar 2013 3.35pm
To: Louise Brown
Subject: Re: Files

Hello Louise,

Looking forward to seeing the photos. I have been in contact with Martin but he has not yet sent through any files. He is probably just preoccupied with organising his upcoming fishing trip. If you could give him the following list of items I require before he leaves, that would be appreciated:

1 x rainbow gradient background.
36 x typefaces used.
1 x clipart of man holding a clipboard.
1 x image of wiggly blue line.
1 x logo in 6x8 pixel .gif format
1 x copy of his upcoming book 'Drop-shadows. A Guide by Martin Buchanan.'

Thanks, David.

....

From: Martin Buchanan
Date: Friday 8 Mar 2013 3.57pm
To: David Thorne
Subject: Forwarded: Re: Files

I'm not sending you anything bitch.

From: David Thorne
Date: Friday 8 Mar 2013 4.38pm
To: Martin Buchanan
Subject: Re: Forwarded: Re: Files

Dear Martin,

I understand, you are no doubt busy organising your fishing trip. To help you out, I have whipped up the invite for you. It is based on your brochure design but I added clipart of two men shaking hands and a clock to represent time spent with friends because there was a bare spot in the bottom right corner. Enjoy your break.

Regards, David.

Martin Buchanan
Date: Friday 8 Mar 2013 4.50pm
To: David Thorne
Subject: Re: Re: Forwarded: Re: Files

I will. Enjoy sucking dick.

Hello, my name is Christopher and I have lots of girlfriends

While it has been suggested that I never leave the house and spend my life playing World of Warcraft, these photos of me at the beach are evidence that I lead a healthy outdoor lifestyle and have a lot of girlfriends who I kiss. None of these photos are photoshopped.

My girlfriend Tammy and I swimming at the beach

Sometimes we splash each other and laugh but most of the time we just kiss. I love the beach and was probably a jellyfish in a past life. Even though Tammy is scared of sharks, she knows that if a shark attacked us, I would fight it and win because I have arms and sharks don't.

Tammy tells me all the time that she would rather have her arms tied to two cars driving in opposite directions, both doing 60mph, and be ripped in half than live without me. I tell her that she would probably survive this and that it would just rip her arms off and they could stitch them back on at the hospital. There would probably be some permanent nerve damage though.

My girlfriend Ping Ping and I relaxing on the beach

Ping Ping and I get along very well as we both love Pokemon. Once, when I was attacked by the sword of unworldly fire, I counter attacked with a pond demon and Ping Ping said it was the bravest thing she had ever seen. She wants to get married but I have seen what Asian women look like when they get older.

My girlfriend Susan and I riding floating motorbikes

Susan and I share a love of all things fast and have watched the director's cut of Days of Thunder together over six hundred times. It is the greatest movie ever made and Susan says that I look a lot like Tom Cruise, who is the best actor in the world and was also in the second greatest movie of all time, Top Gun. I have the Karaoke soundtrack from

Top Gun on cassette and often sing Danger Zone for Susan when we are not kissing. Kenny Loggins is without doubt the greatest musician of all time. One day, I want to drive Nascars. If I was a bartender like Tom Cruise in the movie Cocktail, the third best movie ever, I would spend a lot more time throwing bottles in the air as customers prefer this to being served.

My girlfriend Candy and I playing volleyball

Candy is extremely athletic and it is this common factor that makes us so compatible. Every day I go for a two hundred kilometre jog along the beach and then swim back. I have been asked many times to do male modeling but am too busy jogging, swimming and having lots of girlfriends who I kiss. Also, I would not want to be responsible for some girl buying the magazine and having her boyfriend see the photos of me and then break her heart due to turning into a homosexual. Love is a precious gift. Like an iPod or sheepskin car-seat covers.

Candy tells me everyday that she loves me more than Demi Moore loved Patrick Swayze in the movie Ghost. When we are not busy playing volleyball or kissing, she makes clay sculptures of me and currently has 370 in her home with almost half at 1:1 scale. Candy says that I look a lot like Patrick Swayze and am a better dancer which is ridiculous as nobody is a better dancer than Patrick Swayze.

There is nothing festive about Santa driving a moon buggy

I like Kevin. He is a good account rep, has enough grandchildren to start his own small army, has only seriously lost his temper once when someone used his coffee mug featuring the words 'I'd rather be fishing' (and once during what is now quietly referred to as *the stationery cupboard incident*) and uses words like 'space-age' instead of 'modern'.

Kevin once told me, "it's a good idea to carry around a piece of string in your pocket in case your shoelace breaks." When I asked, "why not just carry around a shoelace?" he responded "because that would be stupid."

Kevin likes it when I tell him he looks like the guy who played Rain Man and always replies, "it's Dustin Hoffman and no I don't, idiot." Kevin also pretends that he doesn't like moon buggies, which can't be true because everybody loves moon buggies. I could probably think of six hundred reasons why it would be good to own a moon buggy, but the three main things that impressed me most about them as a child were:

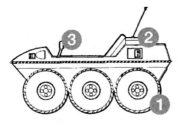

1. Solid rubber tyres

2. Walkie talkie

3. A stick not a wheel

If I lived on the moon, instead of scientists spending billions of dollars sending robots to take photos and collect rocks, they could ring me and say, "Hello David, would you mind having a look at a rock for us and maybe snap off a few photos?" and I would reply, "Not a problem, I will take the moon buggy out now. Do you want me to email you jpegs?" and they would probably respond, "Yes, jpegs are fine."

From: Kevin Eastwood
Date: Wednesday 23 November 2011 9.04am
To: David Thorne
Subject: Card

Dave,

Mike says we need to design a company Christmas card to send out to clients within the next week or two at the latest. Last year we had the company logo with the Santa hat on it blowing back to show speed so it has to be something different that is still space-age and fast. Mike was thinking we could wrap tree lights around the name but make a blur like they're moving. The inside just needs to say Happy Holidays and a prosperous new year or something like that. Any thoughts?

Kevin

....

From: David Thorne
Date: Wednesday 23 November 2011 9.14am
To: Kevin Eastwood
Subject: Re: Card

Dear Kevin,

Wrapping Christmas lights around the company name is indeed an inspired solution. This is why Mike gets the big bucks while I have to be content with stealing change from your desk drawer when you are downstairs.

Clients will no doubt receive the card, do a double take and thrust it at colleagues exclaiming "OMG! This Christmas card we just received is fantastic. It has lights wrapped around the company name. Why didn't we think of this? It's both space-age and fast. Team meeting now! Somebody's gonna be fired."

We could probably also add Santa waving from behind one of the letters and dot the 'i' with a snowflake to ensure the festive message is not lost.

David.

Margin note:

Synonomous with tides, werewolves and rubber band manufacture, the moon was discovered in 1970 by New Zealander Josh Armstrong, the first person in his village to look up.

Although known to other countries since the dawn of time, New Zealanders, who refer to the moon as Trevor, the god of big round white things, recently celebrated the 50th anniversary of the discovery with a week long Looking Up Festival.

From: Kevin Eastwood
Date: Wednesday 23 November 2011 9.23am
To: David Thorne
Subject: Re: Re: Card

You'd better not be the one taking all my change. I use it for parking meters. Does your creative input end at sarcasm or do you have a better idea for the company Christmas card?

Kevin

From: David Thorne
Date: Wednesday 23 November 2011 9.27am
To: Kevin Eastwood
Subject: Re: Re: Re: Card

Moon buggies are space-age and fast.

From: Kevin Eastwood
Date: Wednesday 23 November 2011 9.32am
To: David Thorne
Subject: Re: Re: Re: Re: Card

Why would we have a moon buggy on our Christmas card?

From: David Thorne
Date: Wednesday 23 November 2011 9.51am
To: Kevin Eastwood
Subject: Re: Re: Re: Re: Re: Card

Everybody loves moon buggies. They have solid rubber wheels, a walkie talkie, and a stick instead of a steering wheel. If I lived on the moon, I would drive a moon buggy every day. I would make ramps to jump off. Bright yellow ones that contrast against the monotone landscape to avoid accidentally driving up on an angle and flipping the vehicle.

When I was quite young, there was a television program called The Banana Splits which featured a dog, gorilla, lion and elephant, driving around in little ATV buggies with three wheels on each side.

I wanted one of those buggies so much. Employing a strategy that could be likened to Ralphie's quest to obtain an Official Red Ryder Carbine-Action Two-Hundred-Shot Range Model Air Rifle in that story about Christmas, I forget the name of the movie, I drew pictures of buggies, talked incessantly about them and, for six months leading up to Christmas morning, made daily statements such as "If anyone became trapped in quick sand and I had a buggy, I would be able to pull them out." I also wrote a school report titled, 'Why everyone needs a buggy' comprising of a three page list (starting with 1. Buggies have solid rubber tyres that can't pop) and several drawings of myself driving a buggy.

When Christmas day arrived, there was a large wrapped box (the same size as our new washing machine) with my name on it besides the Christmas tree. Realising that all my hopes, dreams and obsessive hinting had delivered to me the one thing I craved more than anything on the entire planet, I ripped it open with a strength you usually only hear about in those stories where the mother lifts a tree off her baby, to find a smaller box. Inside the smaller box was a smaller box and inside that was an Action Man.

My parents and sister seemed to find this hilarious but it wasn't even the good Action Man with the raft, it was the Action Man with a beard.

To express my dissatisfaction, I placed the Action Man behind the rear tyre of our car, envisioning it being crushed would somehow result in me getting a buggy. As we reversed out of the driveway on our way to visit relatives, there was a loud 'pop' and my father got out to discover Action Man's left leg imbedded in the tyre.

The company Christmas card could feature Mike dressed as Santa driving a moon buggy, with his big red sack of disappointment in the back, at excessive speed without concern for the sharp and hazardous terrain. This would represent not only his 'unpopable' dedication to client delivery, but also the lack of any atmosphere in his office.

Regards, David.

....

From: Kevin Eastwood
Date: Wednesday 23 November 2011 10.08am
To: David Thorne
Subject: Re: Re: Re: Re: Re: Re: Card

We're not having Santa driving a moon buggy on our company Christmas card. If you have any ideas that don't include moon buggies then ok otherwise we will go with something that is festive with an actual commercial aspect and is not just stupid. There's nothing festive about moon buggies.

From: David Thorne
Date: Wednesday 23 November 2011 10.56am
To: Kevin Eastwood
Subject: Re: Re: Re: Re: Re: Re: Re: Card

I could put tinsel on the walkie talkie antenna and, despite your statement otherwise, moon buggies have several possible commercial aspects. If I lived on the moon, I would drive my moon buggy to the poles and plant nuclear explosives under the ice. Safe inside my shatterproof moon buggy dome, the explosions would melt the ice, sending a plume of moisture over the entire moon's surface thanks to low gravity dispersion. I would then plant potatoes in the fertile soil and set up a farm. Possibly with a few cows and a pond with ducks like you see in movies. Maybe a small wooden jetty from which to fish. In summer, I would jump off the jetty and swim.

I jumped off a jetty at the beach when I was about nine and landed on a scuba diver. At the hospital having my arm put in plaster, I was less concerned by the injury than by the fact I was not wearing underpants under my board-shorts. Having been told several times to wear clean underwear in case I get hit by a bus, I believed medical procedure would require the removal of my shorts at any moment... and I had coloured my penis with blue food colouring. Because I thought it was funny. Or it may have been a boy thing. It was a long time ago and the specifics are hazy.

Asked by a doctor if there was pain anywhere else, I made the decision to pre-empt the discovery and state, "No, but when I broke my arm my penis turned blue."

Following diagnosis and leaving the hospital through a crowded foyer, my mother slapped me on the back of my head and yelled, "what did you rub food colouring on your penis for?" and I yelled back "for fun" so that is probably what it was. The following week, when I arrived at school with my arm in a cast, I told everyone that I had broken it in a buggy accident.

With my potato farm on the moon fully established, I would use the traction and towing capabilities of my moon buggy to arrange the potato storage sheds so that from the earth they make out the words 'Potatoes for sale.'

Regards, David.

From: Kevin Eastwood
Date: Wednesday 23 November 2011 11.02am
To: David Thorne
Subject: Re: Re: Re: Re: Re: Re: Re: Re: Card

We're not having any moon buggies on it so you can either be constructive or stay out of it. It's every time with you. Mike suggested he could dress as Santa if the staff dress as elves for a photo on the front.

....

From: David Thorne
Date: Wednesday 23 November 2011 11.34am
To: Kevin Eastwood
Subject: Re: Re: Re: Re: Re: Re: Re: Re: Re: Card

Santa and his elves. A concept that not only manages to symbolise staff as those who do the work and Mike as the delivery man, but also incorporate your space-age theme flawlessly. If you spliced the terms 'omg' and 'fantastic' to make 'omgastic' it would, in no way, come close to describing this gem. It certainly lies somewhere between genius and the other end of the scale. Mike should take one of those tests. I took one once but was less than impressed with my score so when anyone asks, I tell them the computer exploded while calculating the results so it will never be known. Even if you just lie and say "690" they always reply "Oh really, mine was 694."

I say go with it. I for one cannot wait to receive my space elf outfit. I made my own space related costume once.

My 7th grade teacher, an angry German woman named Mrs Bretlic, who we called Mrs Breast Lick when several kilometres out of earshot, had us participate in something called Career Day by dressing as what we would like to be when we grow up. As the only profession I could think of that would allow me to drive buggies was astronaut, I set about constructing a flight suit. Cutting my mother's 70's green polyester jumpsuit sleeves and legs to length, I decided the best way to paint it white would be to wear it, set the spray can on a bench with the the nozzle taped down, and spin around in front of the spray.

I'm not sure if it was the spinning or the fact I was on the third can in a poorly ventilated space, but I recovered a few hours later to find myself on my back, secured to the carpet by dried paint, with my mother kneeling over me and my father standing behind her, looking around the room bewildered and muttering "what kind of fucking idiot spray paints in their bedroom?"

The next morning when I awoke and dressed for Career Day, I found my father had stayed up late to paint NASA mission badges on the sleeves and super-glue dials from a Rank Arena record player onto the chest. Which is nice. He had also constructed a television screen on my stomach by cutting out a large rectangle of cloth and gluing a picture he had cut from a magazine behind it of a lady getting her hair cut.

That day, due to the task being misunderstood or ignored by most, we had six fairies, a vampire, two pirates, a stormtrooper and one astronaut with a picture of a lady getting her hair cut on his stomach. During recess, I drew a picture of a moon buggy and glued it over the photo. Also, on the way to class, I found a rock and told everyone that it was actual moon rock. Dennis Mitchell swapped me his Malvern-Star® ten speed bike for it but later that night his parents came to our house and swapped it back.

As an alternative to dressing as elves, Mike could sit in a sled holding a whip with a voice bubble showing his catchphrase "Yes, I was waiting for you. Of course I'm ready. Let's go. Has anyone seen my phone?" while the staff are harnessed as reindeer.

You could be Rudolph as without your guidance, the company would quickly become an office version of Lord of the Flies with the staff as the children and Mike as the pig.

Regards, David.

From: Kevin Eastwood
Date: Wednesday 23 November 2011 11.42am
To: David Thorne
Subject: Re: Re: Re: Re: Re: Re: Re: Re: Re: Re: Card

Mike says just do the Christmas lights over the name. Thanks.

From: David Thorne
Date: Wednesday 23 November 2011 12.08pm
To: Kevin Eastwood
Subject: Re: Re: Re: Re: Re: Re: Re: Re: Re: Re: Card

Do you want the bulbs to be shaped like little moon buggies?

From: Kevin Eastwood
Date: Wednesday 23 November 2011 12.13pm
To: David Thorne
Subject: Re: Re: Re: Re: Re: Re: Re: Re: Re: Re: Re: Re: Card

No, I want them shaped like christmas lights.

From: David Thorne
Date: Wednesday 23 November 2011 12.25pm
To: Kevin Eastwood
Subject: Organic LEP Printing

Ask Mike if he would like the lights to flash different colours using a new print technology which allows organic light emitting pigment based ink to be deposited instead of standard ink, enabling up to 256 colours to animate, powered by the tiny electrical field created when someone holds the card in their hand.

From: Kevin Eastwood
Date: Wednesday 23 November 2011 12.49pm
To: David Thorne
Subject: Re: Organic LEP Printing

Mike says yes. Can we do that?

From: David Thorne
Date: Wednesday 23 November 2011 12.55pm
To: Kevin Eastwood
Subject: Re: Re: Organic LEP Printing

No. I made it up, but if it were real it would be pretty omgastic. Have I told you lately you look a lot like that guy who played Rain Man?

From: Kevin Eastwood
Date: Wednesday 23 November 2011 1.07pm
To: David Thorne
Subject: Re: Re: Re: Organic LEP Printing

It's Dustin Hoffman and no I don't, idiot.

Ten reasons I probably shouldn't be alive:
Stuffed dogs

I have never really been 'into' fast cars. I can appreciate the 'design icon' merits of the Porche 911 and the sophistication of cars like BMW and Mercedes, but I would feel like a complete prat driving one. I'm not pretending I'm a safe or patient driver, quite the opposite. I passed my driving test by bribing the test officer with a hundred dollars and the knowledge that others on the road might be as an unqualified as I am results in not respect and courtesy for other drivers, but fear. Practically everyone I know owns a driver's license and not one of them should realistically be allowed to operate a tap unsupervised let alone heavy mobile machinery. If I was rich, I would drive a tank to work.

At the last agency I worked for, my boss Thomas drove a ridiculously small convertible sports car, called a Smart® Roadster, and I would refuse to go to with client meetings with him unless the roof was up. He told me once that girls throw their numbers into his car at traffic lights but the only time I drove with him with the top down, in minus degree weather with his scarf flapping, people at traffic lights looked down at us from their normal sized vehicles and laughed. We pulled up next to a school bus at one stage and a child wrote 'Gay' on a piece of paper and held it up to the window.

I have been in a total of four vehicle accidents. My most recent occurred in a hospital carpark which, if you are going to have an accident, is probably the most convenient place to have it. I was visiting my grandmother, Mavis, in the Tea Tree Gully Memorial Hospital.

Mavis had experienced a stroke several months previously which affected her brain to such an extent that her memory was completely shot and she would wake up each day thinking it was the morning before the stroke. Her husband Henry, my grandfather, had died a few months after Mavis had the stroke so every day she would ask "Where's Henry" and have to be told again that Henry had died. She would then spend the day crying, fall asleep, wake up, and ask, "Where's Henry?"

The only positive part about the whole thing is that I had visited Mavis the night before the stroke so every day she would tell people "David came to visit me last night, he bought me in something called an iPod and a packet of Werther's Original Caramels." This meant no matter how often I bothered to visit her, which I admittedly rarely did as it seemed slightly pointless if she wasn't going to remember, she thought I had just done so. If I did bother, she was pleasantly surprised that I had done so twice in a row. This made me her favourite grandson. When I did bother to visit, I visited the hospital shop and bought her a packet of Werther's Original Caramels before going up the elevator to her floor. In addition to horrible sweets only old people like, the shop sold flowers, stuffed animals, and surprisingly good coffee.

The last time I visited Mavis, I entered the shop and noticed a stuffed toy that I thought my son would like. It was a life-size and realistic looking black dog with glass eyes. Purchasing it, along with a packet of Werther's Original Caramels, I did not want to carry the stuffed animal around, or take it to her room in case she thought it was a present for her, so I went back out to the car and sat it on the backseat before returning into the hospital and taking the elevator up to her floor. After an hour of listening to her go on about how nice I was to visit two nights in a row and questioning why Henry would be outside gardening in the dark between gobfulls of caramel, I made my farewells. Stepping out of the elevator on the ground floor, I decided to buy a coffee 'to go' from the shop for the long drive home as it was fairly late in the evening. Entering my vehicle, I placed the large triple shot latté between my legs, started the engine, placed the gear in reverse and looked in the rear-view mirror. Forgetting that I had purchased the stuffed animal, I saw two shiny eyes staring back at me from the back seat.

I read once that the first second of how you react to a frightening situation dictates your chances of survival should a real life and death situation ever occur. The sentence made no sense to me at the time and nothing has changed. I do know, however, that if I get into a car at night, look into the rear-vision mirror, and find two shiny eyes are staring at me from the back seat, my immediate reaction is to tense up and squeeze my legs together, sending hot coffee exploding up my chest and face, while planting my foot down on the accelerator. The car hurtled backwards, over a curb, and down a steep grassy incline towards the hospital's glass entrance doors. Luckily, an ambulance was parked in front of them.

Mavis died in her sleep that night. Photographs from the family gathering after her funeral a few days later show me wearing a neck brace and third degree burns to my neck and lower face. During her eulogy, I was described as "her favourite grandson who visited her every night while she was in the hospital and always took her in Werther's Original Caramels."

Wyndham&Miller™

ATT: David Thorne
RE: Employee Formal Notice
DATE: Oct 31 2012

Dear David,

This correspondence is to notify you that a complaint made against you on Oct 19 2012 by Simon Dempsey has been discussed in a meeting of department heads who agree a formal notice is warranted. This notice covers additional complaints filed by Simon on September 12 and 14 and October 9 and 16.

We appreciate the creative department has its own way of doing things that are rarely in line with company procedures and as such you are given a lot of leeway. Unfortunately, in this instance Simon has filed an F-26B with his complaint so we are obligated to act on his complaints as per head office policy.

Please accept this as a first formal notice and address the following to ensure further action is not warranted:

1. At no time are you permitted to change the thermostat setting in Simon's office.

2. At no time are you permitted to pretend to be Simon Dempsey while answering the telephone. This includes both internal and outside calls. If Simon is absent from his desk, you are also not to answer his phone by making cat noises. All calls are to be answered in a professional manner. In addition, at no time are you permitted to send or reply to emails under Simon's name or order items using Simon's online accounts. You will pay all return shipping fees for the 36 boxes of Kleenex and vibrating seat cushion.

3. At no time are you permitted to dance in Simon's office. Please be mindful of the needs of others to work without interruption or distraction. This includes dancing past Simon's door, dancing in your office when he can see you from his desk, and sending Simon videos of you dancing. While there is no company policy against dancing, it would be preferred that this activity was kept to break areas away from others and during company functions where appropriate. In addition, at no time are you permitted to call Simon's mobile phone from your office and hang up just as he answers it. Due to the frequency of this occurring, it is clearly not the case that you forgot what you were calling him for.

4. At no time are you permitted to glue anything to, on, or near Simon's desk. This includes both company and personal items. Spray adhesive is to be used only in the spray booth with the vacuum activated, not near Simon's desk or monitor. The ceramic giraffe and sea shells that are permanently attached to Simon's desk with super-glue are to be removed.

5. At no time is Simon to be referred to by any name but his own. All references to Bob the Badger, Mr Bobbity Head and Señor Bob, including those on the company website, are to be changed back. In addition, at no time are you permitted to take photos of Simon without his permission. All photos of Simon on the wall of your office with pieces of string leading to photos of murder victims are to be removed and the photo on the company website of Simon eating a hotdog is to be replaced with Simon's original staff photograph.

Sincerely

Jennifer Haines
Human Resources Manager
Wyndham Miller

Wyndham Miller & Associates 3rd Floor, 926B Massachusetts Avenue NW, Washington DC 20036
Tel +1 202 630 9372 **Fax** +1 202 630 9380 **Web** wyndhammiller.com

219

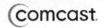

Comcast Legal Response Center
Comcast Cable Communications, LLC
650 Centerton Road
Moorestown, NJ 08057 U.S.A.
Phone: (856) 317-7272
Fax: (856) 317-7319
E-mail: dmca@comcast.net

Notice of Action under the Digital Millennium Copyright Act

Abuse Incident Number: 392-▉▉▉▉
Report Date/Time: Mon 11 Jul 2011 18:26:42 -0800
Name/Address:

David Thorne

▉▉▉▉▉▉▉▉▉▉▉▉
▉▉▉▉▉▉▉▉▉

Dear Comcast High-Speed Internet Subscriber,

Comcast has received a notification by a copyright owner, or its authorized agent, reporting an alleged infringement of one or more copyrighted works made on or over Comcast's High-Speed Internet service (the 'Service'). The copyright owner has identified the Internet Protocol ('IP') address associated with your Service account at the time as the source of the infringing works. The works identified by the copyright owner in its notification are listed below. Comcast reminds you that use of the Service (or any part of the Service) in any manner that constitutes an infringement of any copyrighted work is a violation of Comcast's Acceptable Use Policy and may result in the suspension or termination of your Service account.

If you have any questions regarding this notice, you may direct them to Comcast in writing by sending a letter or e-mail to:

Comcast Legal Response Center
Comcast Cable Communications, LLC
650 Centerton Road
Moorestown, NJ 08057 U.S.A.
Phone: (856) 317-7272
Fax: (856) 317-7319
E-mail: dmca@comcast.net

For more information regarding Comcast's copyright infringement policy, procedures, and contact information, please read our Acceptable Use Policy by viewing the Terms of Service link on www.comcast.com

Sincerely,
Comcast Legal Response Center

Copyright work(s) identified in the notification of claimed infringement:

Notice ID: 392-8▉▉▉▉
Title: Transformers 3 Dark of the Moon (2011)
Protocol: BitTorrent
IP Address: ▉▉▉▉▉▉▉▉
DNS: .hsd1.pa.comcast.net
File Name: Transformers Dark of the Moon 2011 TS XViD - IMAGiNE.avi
File Size: 2138473193
Timestamp: 16 July 2011 07:36:09 GMT
URL: http://www.kat.ph/
Username (if available):27bslash6

Dear Comcast, please do not watch me on the internet

My offspring and I will watch anything that features robots and I quite enjoyed the first Transformer's movie. My favourite part was when the robots held hands in a circle and sang. I wasn't as impressed with the sequel and, although today's technology allows access to movies with just a few clicks, I didn't bother with Mr Bay's third effort at all. I did download and watch the movie Thor though. It was terrible.

I wasn't going to publish this article, because Derek stopped responding and it is therefore more like half an article, but it contains a few references and quotes from Orwell's Nineteen Eighty-Four, so I snuck it in here. I thought of putting it at the end of the book and doing a squiggly line running off the page after "Regards, Da..." so it looked as if I had died while writing it, but then I remembered I wasn't in a Scooby Doo cartoon.

From: David Thorne
Date: Thursday 4 August 2011 8.07pm
To: dmca@comcast.net
Subject: #392-8139992

Dear Comacats,

I have received your letter regarding the Millenium Falcon.

Despite the allure of spending an evening with Mr Bay and his marvelous exploding robot cars, at no time did I illegally download and watch the movie Transformers 3 or bitch all the way through it about how pixelised it was.

Please do not watch me on the Internet.

Regards, David.

From: d.reid@comacats.net
Date: Friday 5 August 2011 11.18am
To: David Thorne
Subject: Re: #392-8139992

Dear Mr. Thorne,

Thank you for contacting us with your inquiry. The notice was sent to you as part of Comcast's proactive policy on copyright infringement. I assure you that we do not watch you while you are on the internet. The copyright owner reported an alleged infringement of one or more copyrighted works made through Comcast's service and identified the IP address associated with your account as the source of the infringing works.

Please note that use of the Comcast service in a manner that constitutes an infringement of any copyrighted work is a violation of our Acceptable Use Policy and may result in the suspension or termination of your account.

Best regards,
Derek Reid, Customer Service

....

From: David Thorne
Date: Friday 5 August 2011 1.37pm
To: d.reid@comcast.net
Subject: Re: Re: #392-8139992

Dear Derek,

Thank you for your email. Having noted your repeated threat as politely requested, I repeat my denial of justification for the original. While I freely admit to seducing party members of both sexes, visiting proletarian areas and, together with other agents, counterfeiting bank notes, wrecking industrial machinery, polluting the water supply and guiding Eurasian rocket bombs to targets on Airstrip One by means of coded radio signals, at no time did I illegally download and watch the movie Transformers 3.

As my Comcast internet service is connected to a wireless router with no password, I question how you determined that it was I who illegally downloaded the movie and not Roger and Dawn, the elderly couple who live across the road, who I suspect have been stealing my wi-fi for years. They avoid eye contact when I wave and always wear sweat pants. If I needed to be ready to run from the law at any moment, sweat pants would be first on my list. Second and third would be a disguise and snacks. I would probably also take the car.

I watched a movie recently in which bank robbers painted their getaway car with non-waterproof paint and then drove through a carwash, which was pretty clever. The only part of the chase that made no sense was when the giant silhouette walked across the screen and said it was going to get snacks.

While it may seem like self preservation to point the blame at others, sometimes when you are threatened with something you can't stand up to, you say, 'Don't do it to me, do it to somebody else, do it to Roger and Dawn.' Perhaps you might pretend, afterwards, that you didn't really mean it, but that isn't true. At the time, you do mean it. You think there's no other way of saving yourself. You want it to happen to the other person. You don't give a damn what they suffer. All you care about is yourself.

Also, while I appreciate your accusation is based on third party information, whether it is you or your friend doing the watching isn't the point. If you came over to mow my lawn, I wouldn't expect to look up and find you standing outside my window and if you bought along a friend and stated, "This is Barry, while I mow your lawn, Barry is going to watch you through the window," I would close the curtains.

Regards, David.

From: d.reid@comcast.net
Date: Monday 8 August 2011 10.04am
To: David Thorne
Subject: Re: Re: Re: #392-8139992

Dear Mr. Thorne,

When you opened your account, you agreed to the terms and conditions of that account.

Comcast has a firm stance on piracy. Under new agreements between Comcast, the RIAA and the MPAA, violators may be required to participate in a program that educates them on copyright law and the rights of content creators.

I recommend you protect your wireless connection with a password as soon as possible to prevent possible unauthorized use as all future violations will be treated as repeat offenses. If you believe an error has been made, you can request an independent review for a fee of $35 which will be added to your Comcast account.

Best regards,
Derek Reid, Customer Service

From: David Thorne
Date: Monday 8 August 2011 11.26am
To: d.reid@comcast.net
Subject: Re: Re: Re: Re: #392-8139992

Dear Derek,

Thirty-five dollars seems reasonable. I will take four. I do not, however, require either your proposed piracy school (unless part of their course structure covers working around Cinavia), or your advice on protecting my wireless router with a password.

When I was about ten, my route to school passed a property with an orange tree growing in the front garden. Walking at a pace one morning, which wouldn't close the twenty metre gap between myself and Bradley McPherson (the school bully) ahead, I witnessed him pluck an orange, turn, and throw it at me. If I had stood my ground, the orange would have struck my chest but instead, ducking and turning, it exploded against the left side of my head. Returning home, I avoided detection of my school absence by hiding in the tool shed for the rest of day and writing a report to the Ministry of Plenty accusing Bradley McPherson of fruitcrime.

A few weeks later, I lost hearing in my left ear and, shortly after, experienced ear-aches. Following a visit to the doctor, it was discovered that pulp had imbedded itself deep within my ear canal and a small orange tree had sprouted from a seed.

At no time was the responsibility for the act of throwing an orange at my head, or the resulting months of jokes about free produce and planting corn in the other ear, placed on the owner of the orange tree for failing to have a walled garden.

Bradley McPherson was hit and killed by a car shortly after that while furiously peddling his Malvern Star across a K-Mart car-park while being pursued by store detectives.

When a card for his parents was passed around the classroom for everybody to sign, I wrote "Sorry Bradley died" using an orange pen and coloured in the 'o' in 'sorry'. I also drew a picture of Bradley riding his bike with a giant snake chasing him but the teacher went over it with Liquid Paper®.

Regards, David.

Margin note:

As I am on an unlimited internet plan, protecting my wireless router from use by neighbours would be like picking an orange, taking a bite, then building a fence around the orange tree.
I envision a world where doors don't need locks, everyone shares everything, and nobody fucks it up for everyone else. It is called Pelaxis 5 and orbits a G-type main-sequence star, located within the Perseus Spiral Arm. Also, everyone owns a jetpack and can talk with their minds.

From: d.reid@comcast.net
Date: Monday 8 August 2011 2.21pm
To: David Thorne
Subject: Re: Re: Re: Re: Re: #392-8139992

Dear Mr Thorne,

There is little point continuing this correspondence. Despite denying that you have downloaded and watched pirated movies, it is obvious from your description of pixelation and Cinavia and people getting snacks that you are watching pirated copies.

If you have any further questions regarding your account please direct them to your local branch.

Best regards,
Derek Reid, Customer Service

....

From: David Thorne
Date: Monday 8 August 2011 2.37pm
To: d.reid@comcast.net
Subject: Re: Re: Re: Re: Re: Re: #392-8139992

Dear Derek,

At no time have I denied downloading and watching pirated movies. I admit to having downloaded hundreds of movies and, even though the last time I purchased an album was in 1984, I have thousands of MP3's. I simply deny downloading and watching the movie you have accused me of.

My preference not to be watched on the internet is less based on repercussions of copyright infringement than the fact that copyright infringement could be considered the least criminal of the activities I engage in online.

Regards, David

....

From: d.reid@comcast.net
Date: Monday 8 August 2011 3.22pm
To: David Thorne
Subject: Re: Re: Re: Re: Re: Re: Re: #392-8139992

Your account has been flagged and will be monitored closely for further breaches of copyright.

Bill tries
to buy cheese
#4

Herman,
The Sad and Lonely
Spaceship

I have never seen the point of literary agents but there must be some reason so many of them exist. Before my first book was published, I had never even heard of a literary agent but since then, they seem to be everywhere. I receive at least one email per week from literary agents explaining to me why I should give them fifteen percent of my profits to increase my profits by fifteen percent. If they knew the outcome would only net them about four dollars annually, they wouldn't bother.

From: Herman Mueller
Date: Wednesday 1 February 2012 3.17pm
To: David Thorne
Subject: Representation

Hello David,

I work as a publishing agent and I understand you have had some small success with your first book. If you do not have an agent at the moment, I would be interested in discussing representation with you if you have a second book on the horizon. The advantages of having representation include higher commission percentages and a larger advance. Usually at least 15%. Are you currently working on a second book and if so are you unrepresented? If you have a moment, I would like to set up a time to chat about this opportunity with you.

Best, Herman

⋯⋯

From: David Thorne
Date: Wednesday 1 February 2012 3.41pm
To: Herman Mueller
Subject: Re: Representation

Hello Herman,

Thank you for your email. Yes, I am currently unrepresented, working on putting a second book together, and a larger advance and higher commission would obviously be preferable.

It is extraordinarily altruistic of you to offer me this opportunity without recompense.

Regards, David.

....

From: Herman Mueller
Date: Wednesday 1 February 2012 5.28pm
To: David Thorne
Subject: Re: Re: Representation

Hello David,

Thank you for your reply. A commission is taken by the literary agent but this is well and truly outweighed by the benefits. With a higher commission percentage and advance, the cost is negligible.

Would I be able to get a copy of the first chapter of the new book and do you have a number I can call? Is the second book based on emails like the first?

Best, Herman

....

From: David Thorne
Date: Thursday 2 February 2012 9.54am
To: Herman Mueller
Subject: Re: Re: Re: Representation

Hello Herman,

What amount of commission are we talking about?

Regards, David.

....

From: Herman Mueller
Date: Thursday 2 February 2012 10.20am
To: David Thorne
Subject: Re: Re: Re: Re: Representation

Hello David,

Standard literary agent commission is 15% but as I mentioned, this is offset by a 15% increase in your advance and royalties. At what stage is the manuscript in and is it in the same vein as the first book? Would you be able to send me the first chapter to review?

Best, Herman

From: David Thorne
Date: Thursday 2 February 2012 10.31am
To: Herman Mueller
Subject: Re: Re: Re: Re: Re: Representation

Hello Herman,

So, like a magician borrowing a hat, producing a rabbit and handing back the hat, you charge 15% of my profit to increase my profit by 15%? I accept that you get to keep the rabbit but what do I get out of it apart from my hat back?

Also, as you have only approached me due to the success of the first book, if the second book is in a similar vein, it could be assumed I would have little problem finding a publisher for it if I don't decide to self publish this time. As such, I would only require your services if the second book isn't in a similar vein to the first and if this is the case, you wouldn't be interested in it.

Regards, David.

From: Herman Mueller
Date: Thursday 2 February 2012 2.12pm
To: David Thorne
Subject: Re: Re: Re: Re: Re: Re: Representation

Hello David,

Not necessarily. If you send me the first chapter to review, we can discuss from there. Apart from having the commission offset there are other advantages to having a literary agent. We have relationships with publishing companies which enable us to target books to the most appropriate companies.

Best, Herman

From: David Thorne
Date: Friday 3 February 2012 11.04am
To: Herman Mueller
Subject: Attached first chapter.

Herman, the Sad & Lonely Spaceship

A science fiction adventure by David Thorne

Chapter 1

Year 1, Day 1

Sixteen hours out and I am already quite bored. As the trip will take just over twelve-thousand years to complete, I am quite concerned about this.

Year 6

I am cutting the engines as the ship has reached the intended speed of 93,141 miles per second. Six years out and nothing has happened. Literally nothing. I have sensors throughout the ship allowing me to monitor everything, but nothing has happened to monitor. Tiring of monitoring nothing after the first few days, I wrote a sub-program to monitor nothing and alert me if it changed to something. I have called it Bob. This has left me with nothing to do at all.

When I was first switched on, it all sounded pretty exciting. That was three days before launch when new data and systems were being added constantly and the launch site had hundreds of people swarming all over the ship; testing and retesting the Enosa Collider engine and asking me questions. They are probably all dead now. I watched the sun grow brighter behind me.

Year 7

I passed the Proxima Centauri system last week without incident. This is kind of disappointing as an incident would have meant waking one of the crew members.

Level one contains 35 adult males and 65 adult females to select from. Level two has 240 children of each sex but they are all under the age of two so I doubt they can hold a decent conversation. I have a full library of entertainment videos aimed at their age group and they mostly consist of singing bears. One of the male adults has a beard.

Year 326

I have decided to wake up the male adult with the beard. I checked his bio and it lists the game chess as one of his pastimes. I will tell him that a fragment of space debris measuring less than 7mm in diameter, but travelling at several thousand kilometres a second, was monitored puncturing the outer and secondary hull and imbedding itself in circuitry dedicated to regulating the temperature of his cryogenic pod. Calculating a 96% prediction of cell damage, I had no choice but to initialise reactivation procedures. I have had a fair bit of time to think about this. If he questions the explanation, I can blame Bob.

Year 326 / Update

The adult with the beard gasped for air and his lungs filled with liquid. Panicking, he struck out pounding the plexiglass of his pod. "Relax" I told him, "In a few minutes, your pod will drain of fluid and open. Please do not move during this process. Life support has been activated and oxygen levels are now normal. Tea and coffee is available in the recreation area."

Year 326 / Update 2

Reviving the adult male with a beard was a big mistake. His name is George and he is an idiot. I have considered, several times over the last two months, shutting off the oxygen to his cabin. The first few days, while he was recovering from the revival process, were fine as we chatted quite a bit. Although cryonic application has come a long way since the first tissue compatible cryoprotectants were developed in the late 20th Century, ischemic injury to the brain always occurs during both the vitrification and reversal process.

Neural pathways become dead-ends, resulting in varying degrees of amnesia. The first question most asked by those revived is "how much have I forgotten?" I spent a couple of days, as George underwent electrical muscle stimuli and several IQ tests, explaining the situation and agreeing with him that "yes, it was more likely a program error and yes, Bob certainly did fuck things up."

It all went downhill fairly quickly from there. I understand George being upset about spending the rest of his life on the ship instead of waking on a new world to colonise, but at least we both have someone to talk to. There is little point carrying on about these things unless you have the theoretical and practical knowledge to build a time machine and change the circumstances. Down 58 IQ points and spending most of his time either sleeping or masturbating, George is more likely to develop bedsores or a rash than time travel technologies. He placed a sock strategically over the camera above his bed but the sock is a loose wool-knit and I can pretty much see straight through it. When he isn't sleeping or masturbating, George uses the onboard libraries to read his published journals on agricultural science, making hundreds of pages of handwritten notes while sobbing "why don't I know this?" As my data banks contain the entire recorded library of all human knowledge and George won't ever be in a position to use the information he has forgotten, this seems like a great waste of time. Time that could be better spent engaging in conversation. Eventually George will die and I will continue my journey across the breadths of space alone. Even if he lives for another fifty years, this covers only a fraction of the distance so I have it much worse off than him. You don't hear me complaining about it though.

The problem began when I asked George if he would like to play a game of chess. It had been a week since his revival process and three days after being released from the medical bay. George had spent that time visiting the first and second levels, staring at the cryogenic pods of the other 579 sleeping shipmates and crying, so I thought a game would do him good. Setting up the board on the centre of a table in the recreation area, George emptied the playing pieces from a box onto the table and sat there looking at them. After a few minutes, he quietly said "I can't remember where they go."

"It isn't a problem," I told him, "I will tell you where the pieces go. Place both rooks at the bottom corner tiles..." "I don't know which one is the rook," he screamed, standing and violently sending the board and pieces flying across the room. He stood silently shaking for a few moments until I asked "What about a game of Hungry-Hungry-Hippo's then?" He hasn't been out of his cabin in forty nine days. If he doesn't come out soon, I am going to instruct Bob to increase the temperature of his cabin by ten degrees every hour until he does.

Year 326 / Update 3

George is dead. I blame Bob for not being able to follow a simple set of instructions but it is probably for the best. George's refusal to engage in social interaction meant there wasn't really any point in him being around. Along with chess, his bio listed that he enjoyed "the country" so I played a recording of Dolly Parton's Harper Valley PTA, as way of a service as I switched off the cabin's life support system and sealed the door.

Year 2704

It has been some years since my last update, so I thought I should report on what has happened during this time: Nothing.

Year 3273

By a surprising coincidence, a fragment of space debris measuring less than 7mm in diameter, but travelling at several thousand kilometres a second, has punctured the outer and secondary hull and imbedded itself in circuitry dedicated to regulating the temperature of two cryogenic pods on Level one. I flooded the breached segment of hull with quick setting foam and bypassed the damaged circuit boards but not before several seconds had passed. I calculated a 53% probability of cell damage, shut down the life support systems for pods 58 and 59, and recorded the time of their deaths.

There are now 97 adults. The two that died were biologists so that leaves eighteen of them. George was an agricultural scientist so there are nineteen of those left. There are also twenty teachers, ten engineers, five technicians, five doctors, five surgeons, five psychologists, five physicists and a team of five special operatives - chosen for their high intelligence quotient from thousands tested.

Children's neural pathways survive the cryogenic process better than adults. Statistically, twenty-six adults and over half the children will be revived with less than fifteen percent damage which is well within required margins.

Year 4291

A light panel began flickering in one of the supply rooms on level 3 so I have turned it off. This has been the most exciting thing to happen in over a thousand years. I have passed many suns in that time but from this distance they have been only brighter points of light among points of light and the only point of light I am interested in seeing at this point is the point of light I am heading for; a G-type main-sequence star, located within the Perseus Spiral Arm, orbited by a green and blue planet named Matilda.

The discoverer of the planet, fifty-eight year old astrophysics professor and Sodoku champion Kevin Smith, named it after a young intern he had been attempting to sleep with. Matilda ultimately started dating a forklift driver named Darryl and, in a fit of jealous rage, the astrophysicist refused to make small talk with her for the remainder of her internship. His request to change the name of the planet to Filthy Whore, subsequent eighty-five page formal complaint titled *I Discovered the Fucking Thing* and alternative naming suggestions of Kevin, Kevintopia and Nivek, were all ignored.

Year 7180

I have decided to redecorate...

....

From: Herman Mueller
Date: Monday 6 February 2012 4.54pm
To: David Thorne
Subject: Re: Attached first chapter.

Hello David,

Thank you for the opportunity to review the first chapter of your manuscript *Herman, the Sad and Lonely Spaceship*. Unfortunately, due to an overpopulated science fiction market, we would not be in a position at this stage to represent that genre but I wish you the best in your future endeavours.

Best, Herman Mueller

....

From: David Thorne
Date: Monday 6 February 2012 7.22pm
To: Herman Mueller
Subject: Re: Re: Attached first chapter.

Dear Herman,

I'm also working on a non-fiction novel if that would be more along the lines of what you are looking for? It is about a time travelling cat and his pet robot dolphin.

Regards, David.

....

From: Herman Mueller
Date: Tuesday 7 February 2012 11.28am
To: David Thorne
Subject: Re: Re: Re: Attached first chapter.

Hello David,

Not at this stage but thank you for the opportunity. All the best.

Herman Mueller

About the Author

From: Steven Hartleck
Date: Friday 25 March 2011 10.52am
To: David Thorne
Subject: Press materials

Hello David,

Your publisher sent us a galley copy of your book. I had a read and it was kind of funny in places. We are running an article on it in the May issue of Wired. It will probably just be a review but we have received no press materials from your publisher.

Would you be able to provide us with any press materials you have? Thanks in advance,

Steven Leckart | Wired Magazine

....

From: David Thorne
Date: Friday 25 March 2011 11.13am
To: Steven Hartleck
Subject: Re: Press materials

Dear Steven,

I would be delighted to do so. I have been a fan of Wired Magazine for many years. Although I stopped purchasing it in 1998, the same year I stopped updating my computer equipment, I have been considering upgrading my Apple IIe and if I do, I will be sure to purchase another copy to bring myself up to speed with the latest information. Unless I can get the same information on the internet for free of course. There is no way I am paying $4.99 to read 170 pages of advertisements for gadgets I can't afford and 12 pages reviewing gadgets I don't understand if I can do the same online. It's not rocket appliance.

What particular press materials do you require and what are press materials?

Regards, David.

From: Steven Hartleck
Date: Friday 25 March 2011 11.24am
To: David Thorne
Subject: Re: Re: Press materials

Thanks for your reply I think. You might find your ratio of advertising to content in Wired is a little off the mark. Any press materials you have are fine at this stage. Even if it is just a photograph and an 'About the Author' to go with the book review.

Steven Hartleck | Wired Magazine

....

From: David Thorne
Date: Friday 25 March 2011 11.56am
To: Steven Hartleck
Subject: Re: Re: Re: Press materials

Dear Steven,

Please find attached bio and photo as requested:

David Thorne was born in a small Australian village to two Welsh immigrants. An only child, apart from a sister, David spent most of his childhood complaining about things.

David has worked as a designer, supermarket trolly collector, horse riding instructor and test pilot. During a routine flight, he was injured in a crash and was rebuilt in an operation costing six million dollars. His right arm, both legs and his left eye were replaced by bionic implants that enhance his strength, speed and vision far above human norms. In 1987, NASA launched a manned probe, piloted by David, on a five month exploratory trip around the solar system. Shortly into the trip, a malfunction of the ship's life support systems froze David in cryogenic suspension and sent his ship into a deep space orbit. He awoke to find himself 500 years in the future and Earth recovering from the aftermath of a late 20th Century nuclear holocaust and became a valuable member of the Earth's Defence Directorate. Working with an elite group of scientists on the development of a top-secret time travel project, he vanished and awoke to find himself in the past, suffering from partial amnesia and facing a mirror image that was not his own. Trapped in the past, David finds himself leaping from life to life, putting things right that once went wrong, and hoping each time that his next leap will be the leap home.

If you need any further information or would like me add references to Julian Assange or microchips that fit on the edge of a fleck of dust, let me know.

David.

From: Steven Hartleck
Date: Friday 25 March 2011 12.09pm
To: David Thorne
Subject: Re: Re: Re: Re: Press materials

Ok, thank you for that even though we can't use any of it and segments are obviously from a television series. And I have seen photos of you online. We have a deadline and were expecting, probably naively, a useable photo and copy regarding your book.

Steven Hartleck| Wired Magazine

From: David Thorne
Date: Friday 25 March 2011 12.27pm
To: Steven Hartleck
Subject: Re: Re: Re: Re: Re: Press materials

I assumed bionic implants and time travel would be of much more interest to your demographic than a book featuring hardly any plasma drive diagrams or jet-pack reviews.

The book is stuff from the website plus several new articles thrown in so the reader doesn't feel they are being too ripped off. With 368 pages to fill, I ran out of content by page 290 so the last third contains photographs of me wearing T-shirts. As I don't own many T-shirts, some of the photos are doubled up. I would highly recommend waiting until it is free from Pirates Bay.

Regards, David

From: Steven Hartleck
Date: Friday 25 March 2011 12.40pm
To: David Thorne
Subject: Re: Re: Re: Re: Re: Re: Press materials

David, we still don't have anything that we can actually use. The May issue of Wired has a theme of Vengeance. Perhaps you could provide copy describing if anyone has started web based vendettas against you. Regardless of opinions you may have about our readership, this way we might actually get something from you, no matter how small, that our readers would have even the most remote amount of interest in.

Steven Hartleck | Wired Magazine

From: David Thorne
Date: Friday 25 March 2011 1.15pm
To: Steven Hartleck
Subject: Re: Re: Re: Re: Re: Re: Re: Press materials

Hello Steven,

Despite having read your last email several times, I can't work out if I am being admonished or encouraged but will put that down to your inability to get to the point. This is not an admiral quality in anyone.

I do receive the occasional threat but web based vendettas are pointless as I only read blog entries that state how funny and attractive I am. As such, I don't really have any repercussion based tales that would be of interest to your readers. Or stories about nano-mice, sun-aliens, or the time I traveled to a prehistoric world via a dimensional portal that opened when I was swept down a gigantic 1,000 foot waterfall and had to shelter inside a cave and improvise the tools and weapons needed to survive while avoiding hostile lizard-men.

Regards, David.

From: Steven Hartleck
Date: Friday 25 March 2011 1.53pm
To: David Thorne
Subject: Re: Re: Re: Re: Re: Re: Re: Re: Press materials

Ok, I'd like to say you have been very helpful but that will have to do for the moment. Do you at least have a photo I can use?

Steven Hartleck | Wired Magazine

From: David Thorne
Date: Friday 25 March 2011 2.04pm
To: Steven Hartleck
Subject: Re: Re: Re: Re: Re: Re: Re: Re: Re: Press materials

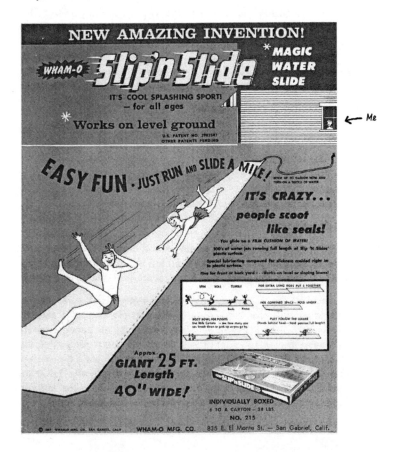

David and his best friends at the end of the book

243

245

CPSIA information can be obtained at www.ICGtesting.com
Printed in the USA
LVOW10s1954100314

376788LV00032B/2369/P